BRITISH AND IRISH AUTHORS

Introductory critical studies

JOHN KEATS

This book offers a revaluation of Keats's major poetry. It reveals how Keats's work is both an oblique criticism of the dominant attitudes to literature, sexuality, religion, and politics in his period, and a powerful critique of the claims of the imagination. For all that he shares the optimistic humanism of progressives like Hazlitt, Leigh Hunt, and Shelley, Keats nevertheless questions the sufficiency of either Art or Beauty.

Professor Barnard shows how the notorious attack on Keats as a Cockney poet was motivated by class and political bias. He analyses the problems facing Keats as a second generation Romantic, his continuing difficulty in finding an appropriate style for 'Poesy', and his uncertain judgement of his own work. The ambiguities and stresses evident in the poetry's treatment of women and sexual love are seen to reflect divisions in Keats and in his society. The maturing use of myth from *Poems* (1817) to *The Fall of Hyperion*, and the achievement of the major odes, are set in relation to Keats's whole career.

BRITISH AND IRISH AUTHORS
Introductory critical studies

In the same series:

John Batchelor *H. G. Wells*
Richard Dutton *Ben Jonson: to the first folio*
Patrick Parrinder *James Joyce*
Robert Wilcher *Andrew Marvell*
Simon Varey *Henry Fielding*
Jocelyn Harris *Samuel Richardson*

JOHN KEATS

JOHN BARNARD

*Professor of English Literature,
University of Leeds*

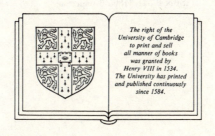

The right of the
University of Cambridge
to print and sell
all manner of books
was granted by
Henry VIII in 1534.
The University has printed
and published continuously
since 1584.

CAMBRIDGE UNIVERSITY PRESS

CAMBRIDGE

LONDON   NEW YORK   NEW ROCHELLE

MELBOURNE   SYDNEY

Published by the Press Syndicate of the University of Cambridge
The Pitt Building, Trumpington Street, Cambridge CB2 1RP
32 East 57th Street, New York, NY 10022, USA
10 Stamford Road, Oakleigh, Melbourne 3166, Australia

First published 1987

Printed in Great Britain at
the University Press, Cambridge

British Library cataloguing in publication data
Barnard, John, *1936–*
John Keats. – (British and Irish authors)
1. Keats, John, *1795–1821* – Criticism
and interpretation
I. Title   II. Series
821'.7   PR4837

Library of Congress cataloguing in publication data
Barnard, John, 1936–
John Keats.
(British and Irish authors)
Bibliography.
Includes index.
1. Keats, John, 1795–1821 – Criticism and interpretation.
I. Title.   II. Series.
PR4837.B33   1987   821'.7   86–14740

ISBN 0 521 26691 2 hard covers
ISBN 0 521 31806 8 paperback

GG

To Hermione

Contents

Preface

Keats was a man of fits and starts, more concerned with the truth of the moment than with overall consistency. His friend, the painter Benjamin Haydon, said, disapprovingly, 'One day he was full of an epic Poem! another, epic poems were splendid impositions on the world! & never for two days did he know his own intentions.' Keats's own characterisation of the poet's 'cameleon' nature gives a more accurate account of his recurrent questionings, affirmations, and ambivalences.

A short account of Keats's poems must inevitably simplify. Where Keats preferred a half-truth if it intimated a partly realised truth of greater importance, a critical reading must look for clarity and shape. However, this reading tries to find room for the failures, contradictions, and reachings after a dimly perceived goal, which characterise Keats's development. Its structure is therefore partly chronological, partly thematic, forming a sequence of essays rather than a single argument.

I have attempted to set Keats's work in the context of the debate about the role and nature of poetry conducted in the first two decades of the nineteenth century. This involves more consideration than is usual of the contemporary reception of the early poems and of *Endymion*. Although Keats's major poems reach beyond their immediate historical setting, the urgency and range of his imaginative quest springs directly from the Romantic crisis.

Keats is difficult because he insists upon asking awkward questions about the pretensions of art, and about basic human fears. How is the knowledge that we are to die, probably in pain, to be related to our pleasure in the world and our senses? Are the claims of art and culture no more than palliatives? The ultimate literalness of Keats's mind is that of the common reader. The directness and uncomforting honesty of the questions he proposes allow neither the poet nor his reader to slip past them. As a post-Romantic, the modern reader inhabits the situation defined by the claims and disclaimers of Keats's poetry.

JOHN BARNARD

School of English, University of Leeds, January 1985

Acknowledgements

My account of Keats is based on the foundations prepared by the editorial work of Richard Woodhouse, Hyder E. Rollins, H. W. Garrod, Miriam Allott, and Jack Stillinger. The biographies by Walter Jackson Bate and Robert Gittings were of constant use. Critics I have found helpful are cited in the notes or the text.

My greatest debt is to Hermione Lee for advice, criticism, and comment at the important stages. Professor Timothy Webb, Dr Elizabeth Cook, Sally Rowland, and my publisher, Terence Moore, who all read the draft typescript, helped me greatly with their advice and criticism. I am also grateful to the anonymous reader of *The Keats-Shelley Memorial Bulletin* for shrewd remarks on an earlier account of the 'Ode to Psyche', and to the journal's editor for allowing me to use parts of the article here. For her patience, tact, and accuracy I am deeply indebted to Mrs Anne Tindall.

Finally, I must thank the University of Leeds for the study-leave which allowed me to write this book.

1

An early nineteenth-century poet

> Now all of twenty-one, he'd written nothing
> of moment but one bookish sonnet: 'Much have
> I traveled. . .' Only he hadn't, other
> than as unrequited amateur. How clannish
> the whole hand-to-hand, cliffhanging trade . . .[1]

Keats is a poet of exclusion, perpetually longing for admission to an imagined other world. His first real poem, 'On First Looking into Chapman's Homer', celebrates the discovery of a 'demesne' previously known to him only by report. *Sleep and Poetry* yearns for a time when Keats might himself become a 'glorious denizen' of Poesy's 'wide heaven' (lines 47–9).[2] His poetry was written out of a fierce ambition for fame, with posterity as its judge. This self-dedication to poetry was frequently a source of energy, as well as providing a dangerously solipsistic subject matter, but it could also be overwhelming – 'the Cliff of Poesy Towers above me'[3] he wrote in May 1817. Indeed, at the end of his brief life Keats feared he had 'left no immortal work behind . . . nothing to make my friends proud of my memory' (*Letters*, ii. 263). Even the apparently confident prediction to his brother and sister-in-law made in October 1818, 'I think I shall be among the English Poets after my death' (*Letters*, i. 394), was a response to the vituperative review in *Blackwood's Magazine*. For Keats 'Fame' belonged to futurity, not the literary politics of his day.

Keats is the only major English Romantic poet whose primary concern is with the truth of Beauty and Art: he told Fanny Brawne, 'I have lov'd the principle of beauty in all things' (*Letters*, ii. 263). His aesthetic ideals, which look back to the classical past, might suggest that his poetry is about what is irrecoverably lost. But Keats's vision of the past is a claim for the centrality of art and imagination in the present, and is a vision of human potential and of the future. Writing in an age which he, like others, believed to be sharply antipathetic to poetry and imaginative truth, Keats attempted to use myth (as did Shelley and Peacock) and romance not as fashionably decorative pass-times but as serious poetic

1

forms. However, the greatness of Keats turns upon his inability to take his own beliefs at face value. Beauty is, perhaps, not even a sufficient truth, let alone the whole truth.

The twentieth-century's recognition of Keats's status as poet and letter-writer, the brevity of his career, and the poetry's striving to attain timelessness, all emphasise the astonishing self-motivation which led to his swift development into maturity. Keats's rapid growth *is* remarkable, but he was also a product of his background and of Regency culture. His poetry needs to be seen in terms of the pressures and influences upon a young poet writing in the second decade of the nineteenth century.

Keats was born on 31 October 1795 in Moorfields, and grew up a Londoner. His father, Thomas Keats, sometimes described as an ostler, in fact managed the Swan and Hoop livery stables. He took the lease over from his father-in-law, who retired to Ponder's End with a modest fortune. Keats came, that is, from a relatively well-to-do family, whose prosperity was based on trade and business. A sign of the young family's sense of its social standing is that his mother wanted to send her sons to Harrow.

In the event, Keats and his brother George were sent to board at the small academy run by John Clarke at Enfield. Keats's stay there from 1803 to 1811 gave him a sound education, one which encouraged a tolerant attitude in religion, an interest in the arts, and a liberal political stance. Keats differed from the other pupils in two respects. First, he developed a passion for poetry which was encouraged by the headmaster's son, Charles Cowden Clarke. Second, his emotional and financial security was threatened by events within his family. His father's sudden death in 1804, when Keats was eight, was followed by his mother's hasty remarriage and temporary separation from her four children. Only six years later she died of tuberculosis, nursed by Keats. The children's grandmother attempted to secure their future by settling money upon them, and appointed Richard Abbey, a City tea merchant, as trustee and guardian. She made over some £9,000 to the orphans. Keats should have received perhaps as much as £2,500 (at the least £1,200) at a time when it was possible to live on £50 a year, and to live reasonably well on £200.[4] Legal wranglings in Chancery kept the money tied up until after his death. In the meantime, Abbey apprenticed Keats to Thomas Hammond, a surgeon, in 1811. Keats successfully completed his professional training in 1816, spending the final year at Guy's Hospital.

Keats was twenty. He could not know that his brother Tom

would die, also of tuberculosis, in 1819, or that the same disease would lead to his own death at twenty six. Freed of his apprenticeship, with a career to fall back on, and believing that his inheritance would shortly allow him an important degree of financial independence, Keats quickly found himself moving in literary and artistic circles which shared his aesthetic beliefs and political sympathies. Although always sensitive to any signs of social condescension, Keats clearly felt himself the equal of the intellectual group made up of men like Leigh Hunt and William Hazlitt. He certainly regarded himself as superior to the *petit bourgeois* – 'Look at our Cheapside Trademans sons and daughters – only fit to be taken off by a plague' (*Letters*, ii. 244–5). When Keats described himself in June 1820 as standing on 'disadvantageous ground . . . in society' (*Letters*, ii. 298), he did not mean that he was an *arriviste*, but that the continued failure of his inheritance to materialise, the critical and commercial failure of his poetry, and his engagement to Fanny Brawne, placed him in an impossible financial situation. Keats's assumption is that he belonged by right to 'society'.

Definition of the middle class is always imprecise, especially when used anachronistically, but it is clear that Keats belonged to the less wealthy part of what would now be seen as the middle classes. In early nineteenth-century England, and in London in particular, the Industrial Revolution, coupled with the growth of commerce and international trade throughout the eighteenth century, had led to a great increase in the number of people employed in the professions, in business, and in trade. Educated and, if successful, financially independent, this quickly growing group had neither inherited rank nor, usually, a university education. Even in the countryside, the old allegiance of squire and clergy no longer represented 'society'. Jane Austen's novels depict a society in flux, with the new middle classes moving towards equality in wealth and social position with the rural, landowning gentry. Keats's scorn for the 'Cheapside Tradesman' is directed at the pretensions to culture of mere shopkeepers: from the viewpoint of a university educated member of the established middle and upper classes, Keats himself could seem equally pretentious. If the expansion of the middle classes created sharp tensions between its constituent parts, the enlarged market for furniture, art, music, and literature made earlier certainties about 'taste' and 'sensibility' seem increasingly uncertain.

Keats himself is representative of, and in some sense a spokesman for, this new 'middle class' audience for poetry, literature, and art. When in August 1818 *Blackwood's* notorious review (probably Lockhart aided by Wilson) placed Keats in Leigh Hunt's 'Cockney School of Poetry' and advised him that 'It is a better and wiser thing to be a starved apothecary than a starved poet; so back to the shop Mr John, back to "plasters, pills, and ointment boxes,"'[5] the savagery was directed by strong social and political prejudices. For the Tory reviewers of *Blackwood's, The Quarterly* and *The British Critic*, Keats was a lower class pretender to culture, presumptuous in writing poetry at all. The use of Greek mythology by someone with no university or classical education was regarded as ludicrous, and the obscurity of his compressed imagery was assumed to stem from Keats's ignorance of poetic technique. Worse, the 'apothecary' wrote about sexuality.

Mr Keats is not contented with a half initiation into the school he has chosen. And he can strike from unmeaning absurdity into the gross slang of voluptuousness, with as much skill as the worthy prototype [Leigh Hunt] whom he has selected.[6]

The same reviewer in *The British Critic* remarked on 'a jacobinical apostrophe' at the start of Book III of *Endymion*, while *Blackwood's* took the lines as demonstrating that the Cockney 'bantling has already learned to lisp sedition'.[7] The upstart poet was also dangerously liberal in his politics.

While it is true that Keats, after an early period of admiration, distanced himself from Hunt, reviewers were right to couple their names. Hunt's *Examiner*, where Keats's first published poem appeared, took a firm reformist political stance (Hunt was imprisoned from 1813 to 1815 for an article attacking the Prince Regent), and the journal was aimed at informing, entertaining, and educating an audience outside those catered for by the conservative *Blackwood's* or *The Edinburgh Magazine* – the latter, though politically liberal, reflected the largely Augustan literary values of its editor, Francis Jeffrey.

The Examiner, edited by Hunt from 1808 to 1821, was only one of a large number of periodicals being published at the time. Many were short-lived, but all mediated a political and cultural position for their audience, and did so from differing standpoints, while the more established literary reviews had a decisive effect on what was bought by the public and by circulating libraries. Although *The Examiner*'s circulation had dropped to about 4,000 by 1817 and 1818 (compared with the 12 to 14,000 of *The Quar-*

terly), its editorial policy attracted readers opposed to the political and literary establishment.[8] One of its subscribers was the head-master of Keats's Enfield school, John Clarke, whose son lent Keats his father's copies. Charles Cowden Clarke later said that Keats's school-boy reading of *The Examiner*, together with the advocacy of religious toleration he found in Burnet's *History*, 'no doubt laid the foundation of his love of civil and religious liberty'.[9] When Keats's first volume appeared in 1817 with a dedicatory sonnet to Hunt, he inevitably appeared as Hunt's acolyte, the Cockney aspirant to culture and sensibility.

Snobbery and class-consciousness were clearly an important element in the *Blackwood's* attack (and Byron's condescending attitude to Keats's poetry is that of the aristocrat), but the over-reaction to a young poet's first volume indicates that Keats's aspirations had touched a nerve. Keats represented a threat.

The reviews' violently contradictory response to Keats's poetry is indicative of the instability of taste in the years 1817 to 1821. To find Byron sharing the High Church attitude of *The British Critic* to Keats's 'Cockney' temerity in dealing with sexuality demonstrates the confusion of differing aesthetic, political, and social presuppositions which affected the public's response. One cause of this confusion was the widening audience for literature. The reviews themselves were a product of this, since the new audience, or rather audiences, needed guidance and education. But that does not explain the violent tone of the rhetoric adopted. Both those reviewers unfavourably disposed towards Keats and some of his later admirers (Shelley's *Adonais* in particular), helped to popularise the *canard* that he was killed by a review. It is a fiction which misrepresents Keats. Lockhart's review in *Blackwood's* did indeed lead to a death, but not that of Keats. In December 1820 the liberal editor of *The London Magazine*, John Scott, published a stinging attack on *Blackwood's* intellectual dishonesty in reviewing the 'Cockney School', characterising the journal as 'The Mohock Magazine'. Scott was challenged to a duel and mortally wounded by Lockhart's friend, Jonathan Christie.[10]

Scott died on behalf of Hunt and Keats. The virulent rhetoric of contemporary critics was an outcome of the deep divisions, political and social, created by the Napoleonic Wars (1807–15) and the rigid political censorship of newspapers, literature, and drama.

All the Tory governments during the war were repressive, terri-fied of Jacobinism or even mild forms of radicalism. The double comedy of Shelley's ineffectually ingenious attempts to circulate seditious pamphlets from Lynmouth in 1812 in bottles thrown into the sea, in miniature boats and hot air balloons, all the time observed by Sidmouth's spies who were reporting his every move back to London,[11] gives an index of the extremities to which the government and radical opposition were forced. It was not until 1822, when Castlereagh committed suicide, and Peel took Sidmouth's place at the Home Office, that any liberalisation occurred. The Peace of 1815, however, promised stability and gave misleading hopes.

Keats's poetry was written, and much of it published, in exactly these years, ones in which change might be hoped for, but had by no means arrived. His own reaction to the political climate of his times is shown by an early outburst, never intended for publication. In 1815 Napoleon escaped from Elba and Louis XVIII fled France to seek refuge in England where he was met by huge crowds. On 29 May bells were rung all over England to commemorate Charles II's restoration. Keats disapproved of both reactions:

> Infatuate Britons, will you still proclaim
> His memory, your direst, foulest shame?
> Nor patriots revere?

> Ah! when I hear each traitorous lying bell,
> 'Tis gallant Sidney's, Russell's, Vane's sad knell,
> That pains my wounded ear.[12]

Support for Louis XVIII was like celebrating the failure of the English Revolution: Sidney, Russell and Vane were all executed for treason against Charles II, and were, like Milton, heroes for Keats, Hazlitt, and Hunt. Hazlitt even saw the defeat of Napoleon at Waterloo as 'the sacred triumph of Kings over mankind'.

What is striking about Keats's poetry, and indeed Hunt's, is how little any of their political convictions appear overtly. This is not entirely due to the danger of censorship. Shelley, a gradualist revolutionary unlike Keats or Hunt, found the threat of prosecution inhibiting, and was forced to express his radical ideas on politics and sexual freedom indirectly through allegory. Hunt, however, made a disabling division between poetry and politics. It would be untrue to say that he believed poetry was mere entertainment inhabiting a purely aesthetic realm (his *Descent of Liberty* published in 1815 is an oblique commentary on the hopes raised by the Peace), but it was a position he came close to adopting in practice. He established *The Indicator* (1819–21), in which Keats's

'La Belle Dame sans Merci' first appeared, as a non-political companion to *The Examiner*, for the recreation and instruction of its readers and as a forum for the kind of literature opposed to that supported by *Blackwood's*. Dickens's portrait of Hunt as Harold Skimpole in *Bleak House* (1852–3), while doing considerably less than justice to Hunt's intelligence as a critic or to his courage as a political commentator, catches Hunt's essential weakness, an ultimately vacuous aestheticism passing over the awkwardnesses of actual life.

The split between the beauty of art and the pain of actuality was Keats's central dilemma: mundane truth is not Beauty. Unlike Hunt, he faced that problem head-on. F. R. Leavis rightly sees Keats as a paradoxical combination of aesthete and realist:

we can ourselves see in Keats (if we can see more too) the great Aesthete – the one Aesthete of genius. For all his unique vitality and creative power, we can see him as related to them by these significantly associated traits which Pater presents: the devotion to exquisite passion and finest senses, the religiose unction of this aestheticism, the cherished pang of transience.[13]

This is essentially true, though it ignores the extent to which Keats's poetry is a comment upon contemporary realities. The heroic gods in *Hyperion* are fighting out the tragic, but finally optimistic, progress towards a better world: *Endymion's* celebration of 'classical' simplicity is partly an indirect reflection on the constrictions of conventional morality and religion. Yet the risk that Keats's 'dreams of art' were an evasion of actuality remains, and was a risk of which Keats was always sharply aware. Throughout, the poetry attests to the extreme tension Keats felt between life and art, but is unable to find any easy or lasting solution.

That tension existed at a very practical level in Keats's day-to-day life. *Blackwood's* was not alone in thinking his choice of career eccentric. Richard Abbey, guardian to the four Keats children, thoroughly disapproved. He even suggested, among other possibilities, that Keats should become a hat-maker. The decision to abandon medicine for poetry was courageous, but not as unrealistic as Abbey thought. His apprenticeship and subsequent training at Guy's, which lasted five years altogether (1811–16), was a professional medical qualification which remained the basis of a possible career. When under pressure to plan a secure future for himself and Fanny Brawne Keats noted that one choice would be to become a surgeon on an Indiaman (*Letters*, ii. 112–13).

Nor was Keats alone among his early friends in attempting to pursue a literary career. G. F. Mathew (1795–?), whose sentimental poeticising Keats briefly admired in 1815, published a few poems and reviews, including a supercilious review of Keats's first volume, in *The European Magazine*. A more substantial example was set by John Hamilton Reynolds (1794–1852), whose *Safie, An Eastern Tale* appeared in 1814. He had published seven works, including *Peter Bell* (1819), by the time Keats died in 1821. Reynolds also reviewed drama for *The Champion* (and arranged for Keats to review Kean's performance as Richard III in that magazine). Although Reynolds's literary career was a failure – he died in 1852, an assistant clerk of the County Court at Newport in the Isle of Wight 'a broken-down, discontented man. . . whose drunken habits placed him beyond the pale of society'[14] – that of Charles Cowden Clarke (1787–1877), who deeply influenced Keats's literary taste while he was at Enfield School and introduced the young poet to Leigh Hunt, was a minor success. Charles Brown (1787–1842), with whom Keats wrote the tragedy, *Otho the Great*, in the closing phase of his life, had his comic opera *Narensky; or, the Road to Yaroslaf* produced at Drury Lane in 1814, which earned him lifelong free admission to the theatre and £300.

These men, like the better-known writers and artists Keats met, Leigh Hunt, Hazlitt, Lamb, or the painter, Benjamin Haydon, had professional or commercial rather than university backgrounds. Brown was a merchant, Reynolds's father was a writing master, Haydon was the son of a Plymouth printer, the father of Lamb was a clerk and servant, Hazlitt came from a Unitarian background and was educated at home, while Hunt, who like Lamb went to school at Christ's hospital, was the son of a preacher. The poor reception and sales of *Poems* (1817) doubtless hurt Keats, but the examples of other members of the Keats's circle showed that his initial failure did not preclude the possibility of ultimate success.

Taylor and Hessey, the young firm which took over *Poems* (1817) from Charles Ollier and became Keats's publishers, believed strongly in Keats's genius, and loaned him both books and money. John Taylor (1781–1864), self-educated son of a bookseller in East Retford who wrote, among other things, a stylistic analysis of Junius, told his father, 'I cannot think [Keats] will fail to become a great Poet.'[15] Taylor's interest in poetry was serious and intelligent, and together he and James Hessey were, as publishers, a mixture of the idealistic and commercial. Their partnership began in 1806, after Taylor had spent a period working in James Lackington's 'Temple of the Muses'. Lackington, an entrepreneur who undercut the prices of his trade rivals, discovered that low prices and a high turnover meant a good profit (in 1781 he was selling 100,000 books a year and retaining £4,000). Lackington believed, with some justification, that there was a new audience for literature. Instead of telling ghost stories on a winter's evening this new public read *Tom Jones* and *Roderick Random* – 'all ranks and degrees now read'.

While Taylor did not learn the lesson about high turnover, he did sense that the market was ready for good new literature. Hence his venture with Hessey. Their policy was to encourage and support the individual writer, and although they did not succeed in making their fortunes, the writers they published, John Clare, Keats, Henry Cary (the translator of Dante), Hazlitt and Lamb, speak for their shrewd literary judgement. In 1821 they bought Baldwin's *London Magazine*, aiming to publish 'genuine original writers' in a review conducted 'on principles of fairness, without any bias from party spirit'.[16] With hindsight it is clear that the hopes for a boom in publishing following the Peace of 1815 was an illusion, but at the time Taylor, Hessey, and others had every reason to believe that imaginative investment would benefit both literature and themselves. Their generosity towards Keats, even when he was seriously ill in 1821, belongs to a relatively short-lived period in which a commercial publisher might expect a poetry list to be a worthwhile area for venture capital.

Taylor and Hessey were optimistic, unrealistically so in the event, but their support for Keats, and indeed Clare, was based on the knowledge that poetry could make money. Even though books were an expensive commodity, the changing audience cut across old boundaries. The market for poetry was considerable, and it was Scott's verse not his novels which laid the basis of his fortune. By 1830 *The Lay of the Last Minstrel* (1805) had sold 44,000 copies, while *The Lady of the Lake* (1810) sold 20,300 in the year of publication, even at the high price of forty-two shillings. In 1804 Venner and Hood paid Robert Bloomfield, 'The Farmer's Boy', 'upwards of 4000£ for his 2 little Volumes'. Byron's *Corsair* (1814) sold 10,000 in its first day on sale, and on 14 February 1819 Keats reported non-committally that Murray had sold 4,000 copies of the fourth canto of *Childe Harold* (*Letters*, ii. 62). With comic exaggeration, Keats said 'Poems are as common as newspapers, and I do not see why it is a greater crime in me than in another to let the verses of a half-fledged brain tumble into the reading-room and drawing room windows' (*Letters*, ii. 130). It was not only the university trained 'polite' reader, with Latin and some Greek, who was reading, but the growing professional middle classes. Cobbett's radical journalism reached an even wider audience. The eighteenth number of his *Political Register*, an 'Address to the Journeymen and Labourers' (2 November 1816) was reissued separately at twopence, and sold 200,000 copies in two months.[17]

Contemporary awareness of this shift was widespread. In 1802 Wordsworth had lamented the modern 'craving for extraordinary incident, which the rapid communication of intelligence hourly gratifies'. Like others, he felt himself to be living in a period of unprecedented change. The modern reader's desire for 'outrageous stimulation' had led, Wordsworth believed, to Shakespeare and Milton being ousted 'by frantic novels, sickly and stupid German Tragedies, and deluges of idle and extravagant stories in verse.'[18] His position, understandably but surprisingly, bears a relationship to the attitude of *Blackwood's* reviewers. Yet Hazlitt, who shared Wordsworth's distaste for 'the prevailing and preposterous rage for novelty',[19] found himself taking a problematic attitude to what he saw going on about him. He was deeply outraged by the perversion of literature's role manifested by Gifford's reviewing of poetry for *The Quarterly*:

This Journal, then, is a depository for every species of political sophistry and personal calumny. There is no abuse or corruption that does not there find a jesuitical palliation or a barefaced vindication. There we meet the slime of hypocrisy, the varnish of courts, the cant of pedantry, the cobwebs of the law, the iron hand of power. Its object is as mischievous as the means by which it is pursued are odious. The intention is to poison the sources of public opinion and individual fame – to pervert literature, from being the natural ally of freedom and humanity, into an engine of priestcraft and despotism, and to undermine the spirit of the English constitution and the independence of the English character.[20]

Good poetry, great literature, were for Hazlitt an inextricable part of human progress towards liberty. The invention of printing was seen by Hazlitt (and by Keats) as a powerful agent of progress. 'There is no doubt, then, that the press (as it has existed in modern times) is the great organ of intellectual improvement and civilisation.'[21] Yet Wordsworth's genius set a problem.

[His Muse] partakes of, and is carried along with, the revolutionary movement of our age: the political changes of the day were the models on which he formed and conducted his poetical experiments. His Muse . . . is a levelling one. It proceeds on a principle of equality, and strives to reduce all things to the same standard.[22]

One kind of liberal radicalism, Hazlitt's, here comes up against the stylistic results of Wordsworth's conservative radicalism in *The Lyrical Ballads*. Wordsworth's levelling of literary language to the 'common man' not only raised the question of what kind of style *was* appropriate for modern poetry, but denied literature's heroic role in creating progress, change, and liberty. Hazlitt saw that his own heroic view of literature implied that if literature were a 'power' then it could be seen as anti-democratic. Hazlitt considered the problem in his reply to Gifford's review of his *Characters of Shakespeare's Plays* (1817), from which Keats quotes extensively and with approval:

the language of Poetry naturally falls in with the language of power . . . Poetry . . . the imagination, generally speaking, delights in power, in strong excitement, as well as in truth, in good, in right, whereas pure reason and the moral sense approve only of the true and good . . . No but we do read with pleasure of the ravages of a beast of prey, and we do so on the . . . same principle that makes us read with admiration and reconciles us in fact to the triumphant progress of the conquerors and mighty Hunters of mankind, who came to stop [written 'stope'] the shepherd's Pipe upon the Mountains and sweep away his listening flock.

(*Letters*, ii. 74–5)

Hazlitt is struggling with the fact that poetry, by its nature, might be on the elitist and authoritarian side: his answer is to say that it is as excited by evil and power as by good. Keats perceived and struggled with the same dilemma, but was continually exercised by Hazlitt's here unadmitted question, 'What role does poetry have in society?' Both Keats and Hazlitt take the longer-term view: poetry, and indeed, art in general cannot be called to account within a particular historical morality or social situation.

Inevitably, this perspective coupled with his treatment by *Blackwood's* left Keats distrustful of both the 'public' and the profession of literature. He badly wanted recognition: he told Fanny Brawne in August 1819, 'if I fail I shall die hard' (*Letters*, ii. 142). But success had to be on his own terms. Both the rejected and published prefaces to *Endymion* are remarkedly ill-judged, for Keats not only tells prospective readers that the poem is inexperienced and immature but says the 'two first books, and indeed the two last, I feel sensible are not of such completion as to warrant their passing the press'. However, the self-dismissal comes from Keats's humility before the great poetry of the past, not from any respect for his public.

> I have not the slightest feel of humility towards the Public – or to any thing in existence, – but the eternal Being, the Principle of Beauty, – and the Memory of great Men – . . . a Preface is written to the Public; a thing I cannot help looking upon as an Enemy, and which I cannot address without feelings of Hostility . . . I never wrote one single Line of Poetry with the least Shadow of public thought. (*Letters*, i. 266–7)

Despite the element of posturing here, Keats never consciously deviated from the belief that his poetry had to be recognised for itself, or from the determination not to court the public.

In reality, his reaction to the 'public' was altogether more complicated. He wrote to Taylor in the summer of 1819 proposing that his share in what he and Brown hoped would be the 'moderate profits' of *Otho the Great* should be used as bond against any money lent by the publisher to the poet. The letter becomes a credo:

> I feel every confidence that if I choose I may be a popular writer; that I will never be; but for all that I will get a livelihood . . . You will observe at the end of this if you put down the Letter 'How a solitarry life engenders pride and egotism!' True: I know it does but this Pride and egotism will enable me to write finer things than any thing else could – so I will indulge it – Just so much as I am hu[m]bled by the genius above my grasp, am I exalted and look with hate and contempt upon the literary world . . . Who would wish to be among the commonplace crowd of the little-famous – whom are each individually lost in a throng made up of themselves? (*Letters*, ii. 144)

Defending this outburst, Woodhouse told the publisher that Keats's letter exhibited literary, not personal pride, a proper pride which would not 'minister to the depraved taste of the age' (*Letters*, ii. 150).

However, pride alone would not pay his debts. Under the financial and emotional pressures of late 1819, Keats oscillated violently between the ideas of giving up poetry, taking up a medical career, and writing for a living. The prospect of becoming a literary journalist is mentioned several times in the letters, usually with distaste, but in a practical way. In September he compared himself to John Hamilton Reynolds, who had turned to the law, but could, Keats thought, have made an income from writing. He goes on:

I will write, on the liberal side of the question, for whoever will pay me.
I have not known yet what it is to be diligent. I purpose living in town
in a cheap lodging, and endeavouring, for a beginning, to get the theatricals
of some paper. When I can afford to compose deliberate poems I will.

(Letters, ii. 176)

Whether or not Keats could have disciplined himself to this mode
of life cannot be known. But Thomas Carlyle, born in the same
year as Keats and from a poorer background, did become a professional man of letters. His first book, *The Life of Frederick Schiller*
(1825), was published by Taylor and Hessey, Keats's own
publishers.

Keats's early determination to 'write independantly' (*Letters*, i.
374) as a poet meant he could not expect popularity, hence the
necessity to think of writing for periodicals and booksellers. It was,
of course, impossible for him or his poetry to be wholly independent of public taste. The case of *The Eve of St Agnes* is revealing.
The poem had been written swiftly in January 1819. When Keats
came to revise it for publication nine months later, he feared that
it was mawkish. He therefore revised the poem making it more
sexually explicit. Taylor was outraged, and threatened not to print
Keats's work unless the original text was restored. Quite apar
from his moral objections, Taylor felt the proposed revisions were
'the most stupid piece of Folly' on two grounds. First, they would
again lead to the neglect or censure from which *Endymion* had suf-
fered – 'He does not bear the ill opinion of the World calmly, &
yet he will not allow it to form a good Opinion of him & his
Writings' (*Letters*, ii. 182). Second, sexual explicitness would
alienate an essential part of the prospective audience:

the flying in the Face of all Decency & Discretion is doubly offensive from
its being accompanied with so preposterous a Conceit on his part of being
able to overcome the best founded Habits of our Nature. – Had he
known truly what the Society and what the Suffrages of Women are
worth, he would never have thought of depriving himself of them.

(Letters, ii. 183)

What worried Taylor was that Keats had told Woodhouse 'that he
does not want ladies to read his poetry: that he writes for men'.
As Tim Chilcott points out, Taylor and Hessey's experience
showed the immense importance of women readers. In 1814 the
advertisement for Ann Taylor's *Practical Hints to Young Females*
defined its expected readership.

Females in the middle ranks of society, in those especially which include
numerous occupations and confined circumstances, are more immedi-

ately addressed; and to them many of the following observations assume to be of essential importance.

Four thousand copies of her book sold in the first ten months, and by 1822 it reached an eleventh edition.[23] Women readers were vital for the success of literature. From a commercial point of view Keats was cutting off his nose to spite his face.

The irony is that Taylor's objections as a publisher and upholder of public morality were right for the wrong reasons. In September 1819 Keats no longer trusted his original inspiration, and was eager to make his poetry 'unsmokeable' by hostile critics: his aim was to avoid the charge of sentimentality, and to make it more 'manly'. What he actually did, through a relatively small number of changes, was to destroy the poem's finely balanced negotiation between innocence and experience. If the public's sense of what constituted good poetry was unstable, Keats's critical perception of his own work was occluded by the same instability.

The episode illustrates the narrow margin between success and failure in much of Keats's poetry. It also shows why 'vulgarity', both of style and content, was a key term for what Keats's contemporary critics found uncomfortable or disturbing in his work: the inclusion of Keats in the canon of English Romantic poetry is an implicit denial of that charge, yet to smooth away or ignore the qualities in the poetry which led critics to accuse it of vulgarity makes Keats seem a less surprising, even a less vital, poet than he is. Keats's 'independence' was essential, despite the recurrent anxieties and difficulties it caused. As he wrote to James Hessey,

The Genius of Poetry must work out its own salvation in a man: It cannot be matured by law & precept, but by sensation & watchfulness in itself – That which is creative must create itself. (*Letters*, i. 374)

2

'Energy and Voluptuousness': *Poems* (1817)

The origins of Keats's ambitions were wholly literary. When Cowden Clarke introduced him, at about sixteen, to Spenser, Keats went through *The Faerie Queene*

'as a young horse would through a spring meadow – ramping!' Like a true poet, too – a poet 'born, not manufactured,' a poet in grain, he especially singled out epithets, for that felicity and power in which Spenser is so eminent. He *hoisted* himself up, and looked burly and dominant, as he said, 'what an image that is – '*sea-shouldering whales!*'[1]

Keats's concern was not with Spenser's depiction of the whale as a 'dreadfull pourtraict of deformitee',[2] but with the way these words enact physical sensation through imagery. He unerringly picked out a phrase which has the power of empathic projection, of physical enactment through words, which marks his mature work. His ability to identify with other states of being is as obvious in his remark to Reynolds –

I lay awake last night – listening to the Rain with a sense of being drown'd and rotted like a grain of wheat –   (*Letters*, i. 273)

as in the more frequently quoted claim by Keats that he could enter into a billiard ball, taking a 'sense of delight from its own roundness, smoothness and very volubility. & the rapidity of its motion' (*Letters*, i. 389). Both these remarks testify to Keats's persistent effort to make the self reach out to otherness through poetry.

Clarke's anecdote illustrates other features of the young Keats. The inwardness and physicality of his response led to an immediate desire to emulate (his first known poem is the weak 'Imitation of Spenser'). A Victorian response to this occasion moves closer to its larger significance. David Masson thought that 'From that moment Keats lived only to read poetry and write it'. Masson's Victorian sentimentalisation provides a valuable insight, for he goes on to say, 'He brooded over fine phrases like a lover'.[3] The early poetry does indeed brood over its 'luxuries', and art too often stands between Keats and life.

15

Even when giving a catalogue of natural beauties (or in the early Keatsian vocabulary, gathering a 'posy / of luxuries, bright, milky, soft and rosy'), literature intervenes. Describing the movement of shadows over a stream, he writes:

> Why, you might read two sonnets, ere they reach
> To where the hurrying freshnesses aye preach
> A natural sermon o'er their pebbly beds . . .
>
> (*I Stood Tip-toe*, lines 69–71)

In the following lines a considerable adjustment of our normal response is required if they are to be read as an effort at empathic description,

> Here are sweet peas, on tip-toe for a flight:
> With wings of gentle flush o'er delicate white,
> And taper fingers catching at all things,
> To bind them all about with tiny rings.
>
> (*ibid.*, lines 57–60)

Seeing and feeling are intermingled, and the reader is at least half-repulsed by a sense that words and rhythms are self-regarding, using the sweet peas as an excuse for poetry. Yet the description means to overleap any concern for conventional verbal decorum in its eager excitement to catch a physical sense of the flower's world. 'Tip-toe', over-used by the young Keats to describe being poised between two states, is too colloquial, and 'taper' is a favourite word of Hunt's, but 'flush' combining feeling and colour at once is characteristically Keatsian. The point is not whether the passage comes off or not, but the oddity of Keats's diction, and the narrow line between success and failure. This also applies to Keats's mature poetry, where familiarity has taken away the sense of surprise at the peculiarities of his poetic language. Byron told Hunt that he found the line 'O for a beaker full of the warm South' unintelligible. While this reflects the deep antipathy between Byron's and Keats's styles, it points to the strain felt by many contemporary readers when faced with Keats's diction. Hunt commented:

It was not the word 'beaker' that troubled him. College had made him intimate enough with that. But the sort of poetry in which he excelled, was not accustomed to these poetical concentrations.[4]

'Warm South' is indeed a 'poetical concentration': grapes, which grow in Mediterranean countries as opposed to the cold North, ripen in late summer, and, when turned into wine, provide bottled 'warm South'. But Hunt's bluff certainty gives only a partial explanation of Byron's difficulties. In context, the next line immediately offers the reader a false lead:

> O for a beaker full of the warm South,
> Full of the true, the blushful Hippocrene.

'True Hippocrene' suggests, at least momentarily, that the 'draught of vintage' is not literally wine but a metaphor standing for poetic inspiration (Hippocrene, the Muses' fountain near mount Helicon, had, according to some authorities,[5] 'violet-coloured' ['blushful'] waters). The local effect is disconcertingly unstable. It is also highly literary. A glass of red wine with 'beaded bubbles winking [!] at the brim' is surprising enough. To have it described in addition as 'a draught of vintage' and as 'the true, the blushful Hippocrene' makes the identification with actual experience even more problematic. Wine and poetry seem interchangeable in the second stanza. Not until the fourth stanza does the ode explicitly reject the god of wine in favour of poetry ('Not charioted by Bacchus and his pards,/ But on the viewless wings of Poesy'). Only then is the reader certain that the earlier identification is ironic. The true Hippocrene is *not* 'blushful wine' (both red itself and the cause of flushing), but poetic inspiration. The pleasures of wine are a simulacrum of the pleasures of Poesy. Byron's confusion is less easily explained away than Hunt allows.

Keats's stylistic success exists in an eerie proximity to vulgarity or technical failure. The early poetry's idiosyncrasy is worth insisting upon because it is integral to the mature work. In 'Ode on a Grecian Urn' phrases like 'ditty of no tone' or 'never bid the Spring adieu' draw on a specialised vocabulary, as distant then as now from common speech, while the exclamatory intensity of a line like

> More happy love! more happy, happy love!

evaporates into the risible when taken out of context. Or again, poetry would normally avoid the juxtaposition of 'up' and 'upon' in

> Long, long those two were postured motionless,
> Like sculpture builded-up upon the grave
> Of their own power.   (*The Fall of Hyperion*, I. 382–4)

yet it has the unthinking inevitability of Shakespeare's

17

> Yet thou doest looke
> Like patience, gazing on King's graves, and smiling
> Extremitie out of act.[6]

With Shakespeare, Keats shares an unconcern towards decorum, a need to take what comes to hand and press it into service. It is what Leigh Hunt characterised as Keats's 'unmisgiving' quality.[7]

But *Poems* (1817) was an ill-judged publication, and, seen in retrospect, premature. It has to be seen from two perspectives, that provided by the later poetry which is highly selective, and that provided by taking the volume on its own terms at this point in Keats's development.

In 1820 Leigh Hunt wrote, 'The character of [Keats's] genius is that of energy and voluptuousness, each able at will to take leave of the other, and possessing, in their union, a high feeling of humanity'[8]. Those qualities, though not under control, can be discerned in *Poems* (1817). 'Energy' appears most frequently when the idea of poetry itself excites Keats. The rapt astonishment, the humble yet heightened awe at discovering Homer's 'realms of gold', captures that sense of enlargement, of entering new worlds, which literature can offer:

> Oft of one wide expanse had I been told
>   That deep-browed Homer ruled as his demesne;
>   Yet did I never breathe its pure serene
> Till I heard Chapman speak out loud and bold:
> Then felt I like some watcher of the skies
>   When a new planet swims into his ken;
> Or like stout Cortez when with eagle eyes
>   He stared at the Pacific – and all his men
> Looked at each other with a wild surmise –
>   Silent, upon a peak in Darien.
>   ('On First Looking into Chapman's Homer', lines 5–14)

The deficiencies – the clumsiness of 'Oft of' or 'felt I like', and, most remarkably, the major error of fact (as Tennyson pointed out 'History requires . . . Balboa' not Cortez)[9] – are absorbed into the generosity of the imaginative tribute, and the rightness here of the poetic 'demesne' and 'pure serene'. The world created by literature is one discovered by the reader, pre-existent, and of heroic and cosmic proportions.

Vitality and energy are also apparent in Keats's self-dedication to literature. In *Sleep and Poetry*, completed at Leigh Hunt's Hampstead cottage in December 1816, Keats asks for

> . . . ten years, that I may overwhelm
> Myself in poesy; so I may do the deed
> That my own soul has to itself decreed.   (lines 96–8)

The strenuous ambition and independence is balanced by a humility that recognises the gap between present and hoped-for abilities ('O Poesy! for thee I hold my pen / That am not yet a glorious denizen / Of thy wide heaven . . .', lines 47–9). Aspiration is coupled with a sense of poetry's power. Given inspiration, Keats foresees the time when

> . . . the events of this wide world I'd seize
> Like a strong giant, and my spirit tease
> Till at its shoulders it should proudly see
> Wings to find out an immortality.   (lines 81–4)

The large scale ('wide world', 'giant') and handling of abstractions as physical entities ('seize events', 'my spirit's . . . shoulders') revitalize the inherited cliché of 'winged poesy'. Yet the oddest word is the prosaic 'tease'. A surprising enough rhyme with 'seize', it is doubly disconcerting coming in the same line as 'giant'. Unexpected, yet inevitable once there, it depends upon bearing the double sense of 'teasing out' (as with wool or an argument) and 'mocking'. The sentiments expressed tread a similarly narrow line as the diction: without the conditional tense ('if . . . I would'), which places this as only a possible (though invigorating) vision, the lines could eaily fall over into self-aggrandising bombast, the kind of gesturing encouraged by his friendship with the painter, Benjamin Haydon, to whom Keats wrote 'The Trumpet of Fame is as a tower of Strength the ambitious bloweth it and is safe' (*Letters*, i. 141).

The use of the conditional and subjunctive throughout the volume signals a fundamental honesty – the poet's large assertions are promissory. They are also accompanied by a prescient sense of his own development, though the stages of that development are callowly imagined. 'Voluptuousness' undermines energy.

> Then will I pass the countries that I see
> In long perspective, and continually
> Taste their pure fountains. First the realm I'll pass

Of Flora, and old Pan: sleep in the grass,
Feed upon apples red, and strawberries,
And choose each pleasure that my fancy sees;
Catch the white-handed nymphs in shady places,
To woo sweet kisses from averted faces –
Play with their fingers, touch their shoulders white
Into a pretty shrinking with a bite
As hard as lips can make it, till, agreed,
A lovely tale of human life we'll read.   (lines 99–110)

This is quintessential early Keats, astonishingly unself-knowing and self-indulgent. The 'apples red' and 'strawberries', intended as metaphors for the beauties and luxuries which the poet's fancy will find, are as disconcertingly physical as the 'nymphs'. After such biting, the reading of poetic tales together coyly turns away from a strongly suggested conclusion. Worse is to come.

And one [nymph] will teach a tame dove how it best
May fan the cool air gently o'er my rest;
Another, bending o'er her nimble tread,
Will set a green robe floating round her head,
And still will dance with ever varied ease,
Smiling upon the flowers and the trees:
Another will entice me on, and on
Through almond blossoms and rich cinnamon;
Till in the bosom of a leafy world
We rest in silence, like two gems upcurled
In the recesses of a pearly shell.   (lines 111–21)

Keats means this passage to be read as an allegory with the nymphs representing various aspects of his poetic muse. The 'realm' of Flora turns out to be a particularly elaborate example of the 'bowers', 'nooks', and 'nests' of 'luxuries' which occur throughout *Poems* (1817). As Mario D'Avanzo has shown, Keats persistently uses the bower or nook both as an analogue for 'the place of poetic inspiration' and as an 'analogue for achieved poetic form,'[10] but here as elsewhere in the volume and in *Endymion* intention and effect slide away from one another. There is indeed an initiation, but hardly a poetic one. The passage is an adolescent male sexual fantasy, mainly one of passive excitement but with hints of aggression ('kisses' becomes 'bites'), and consummation is presumably hinted at by the 'almond blossoms and sweet cinnamon'. The final image of two pearls (?) silent, still yet together, in the haven of a shell, is bodiless and pure, a swift withdrawal from the threat of too realistic an interpretation.

Visions of poetry insistently transform themselves into dreams of sexuality. Any discomfiture here is that of the reader, since the poet seems unaware of these possibilities.

But if the two major statements of this and the next verse paragraph are put together – Keats must first inhabit the realms of Flora and Pan (that is, the early poetry and *Endymion*) before leaving them for a 'nobler life, / Where I may find the agonies, the strife / Of human hearts' (lines 123–5) – the poem gives a wholly accurate account of how Keats was to develop, and of his major concerns. Even here there is a continued strain between intention and effect. Keats's facility at writing, so to speak, pure Keatsian is dangerous. In *Sleep and Poetry* and *I Stood Tip-toe*, the two longest and most ambitious poems in *Poems* (1817), the urge to large statement repeatedly slips off into a catalogue of sensations or 'allegory'. Abstract generalisation and undue particularity are his Scylla and Charybdis. A passage a little later in *Sleep and Poetry* is a good example of Keats caught between the demands of a 'high argument' and the bent of his own genius. He is suggesting that contemporary poets ought to be able to write great poetry, thus re-establishing serious poetry on a level with that of the Elizabethans and Milton after the Augustan perversion and diminution of poetry's role:

> Is there so small a range
> In the present strength of manhood, that the high
> Imagination cannot freely fly
> As she was wont of old? Prepare her steeds,
> Paw up against the light, and do strange deeds
> Upon the clouds? Has she not shown us all?
> From the clear space of ether, to the small
> Breath of new buds unfolding? From the meaning
> Of Jove's large eye-brow, to the tender greening
> Of April meadows? Here her altar shone,
> E'en in this isle; and who could paragon
> *The fervid choir that lifted up a noise*
> *Of harmony, to where it aye will poise*
> *Its mighty self of convoluting sound,*
> *Huge as a planet, and like that roll round,*
> *Eternally around a dizzy void?*
> Ay, in those days the Muses were nigh cloyed
> With honours; nor had any other care
> Than to sing out and soothe their wavy hair.
>
> (lines 163–80; my italics)

21

The opening lines are hortatory and high-minded but limp, while the last three fall back on Muse-as-nymphs imagery. In both these areas Keats seems to be writing on auto-pilot. But the remarkable image of the Elizabethan poets' harmony rolling eternally around 'a dizzy void' is a striking, and strikingly Keatsian, metaphoric construction, self-enclosed, intertwining sound and sight, space and time. Although the metaphor is cast in terms of the visible, sound cannot be literally visualised in this way, which is of course precisely the rhetorical point. The effect is related to Milton's oxymoronic 'darkness visible' which forces the reader to imagine a darkness so dark as to be perceptible. Here the paradoxical mingling of the senses is meant to do more than force the reader into a realisation of the awesome mystery of the choir's sound. It is intended to force us towards an intuitive grasp of the 'etherial' nature of true poetry, to take us beyond normal human limits. The synaesthetic metaphor, deliberately confusing the senses of sound and sight, attempts to embody (or, in Keats's word, 'prefigure') a mode of perception going beyond the rational (the 'consequitive') to one based directly on sensation. The difficulty is that in this context Keats can do nothing with it.

The same sense of cosmic scale produces the one good line in the second sonnet addressed to Haydon, which is otherwise a mixture of the bombastic and coy:

> And other spirits there are standing apart
> Upon the forehead of the age to come. (lines 9–10)

The image is, I take it, of future poets standing on the forehead of the sun-god Apollo, ready to rise above the horizon. Like the previous example, it points forward to the gigantic figures of the Titans in the two versions of *Hyperion*.

The uncomfortable and uneasy elision of classical goddesses with contemporary 'nymphs' is a persistent feature of the early poetry. Keats's sonnet to his brother's fiancée, which was published in *Poems* (1817), begins

> Nymph of the downward smile, and sidelong glance,
> In what diviner moments of the day
> Art thou most lovely?

It concludes,

> But thou to please wert nurtured so completely
> That I can never tell what mood is best.

> I shall as soon pronounce which Grace more neatly
> Trips it before Apollo than the rest.

Interestingly the manuscript fair copy tries out the possibility of replacing 'Grace' with 'Nymph'. In a complimentary poem like this, the fiction is merely silly (though it is also the sign of an attitude to women which idealises their beauty, while regarding their function as merely decorative and made to serve man's pleasure). In the attemptedly serious 'visions' of *Poems* (1817) and in *Endymion*, the confusion is disabling.

Why do classical gods appear in Keats's poetry with such frequency? The superficial answer, which applies to Keats's very earliest poetry, is that it was fashionable for poets to fancy seeing Greek gods in English landscapes. When Keats wrote to G. F. Mathew regretting that his medical studies were keeping him from poetry, he remembers their earlier poetic brotherhood with nostalgia:

> . . . far different cares
> Beckon me sternly from soft 'Lydian airs',
> And hold my faculties so long in thrall,
> That I am oft in doubt whether at all
> I shall again see Phoebus in the morning:
> Or flushed Aurora in the roseate dawning!
> Or a white Naiad in a rippling stream;
> Or a rapt seraph in a moonlight beam;
> Or again witness what with thee I've seen,
> The dew by fairy feet swept from the green.
> ('To George Felton Mathew', lines 17–26)

It was not only Keats and Mathew whose poetic wanderings in the countryside provided such 'visions'. They are to be found in Hunt's poems, and John Hamilton Reynolds, arguing that in *Poems* (1817) Keats sings from 'the pure inspiration of nature', connects precisely this kind of fanciful day-dreaming with, surprisingly for us, Keats's simplicity and truth to nature:

In the simple meadows he has proved that he can

> ' – See shapes of light, aerial lymning,
> And catch soft floating[s] from a faint heard hymning.'
> [*Sleep and Poetry*, lines 33–4]

. . . He relies directly and wholly on nature. He marries poesy to genuine simplicity.[11]

23

This takes the argument back to the 'Cockney School of poetry', whose Greek gods and scenes reflect the same popular taste which appears in many of Wedgwood's designs, in Regency architecture and furniture, and the Empire style in women's clothes. In this idiom, the fashion is decorative, an assertion of bourgeois taste, and a rejection of, an escape from, everyday commercial and urban life. Where Keats differs is in the intense literalness with which he attempted to create, and then believe in, these fictions.

There is a serious side to Keats's mythologising effort, but that is best approached by asking what audience *Poems* (1817) had in mind, and then by examining Keats's views on where poetry stood in 1817. *Poems* (1817) is partly meant as a showcase for a new poet's talents: it also stakes a claim for Keats's place in modern poetry. Attempts at narrative ('Calidore', 'Specimen of an Induction', 'Imitation of Spenser'), verse epistles (to his brother, Cowden Clarke and Mathew), album verse ('To Some Ladies'), apprentice sonnets, an ode ('To Hope'), and the two longer descriptive 'visionary' poems (*I Stood Tiptoe* and *Sleep and Poetry*) demonstrate the young poet's promising variety of forms and styles. Those poems addressed to named or un-named individuals, ranging from Keats's immediate family (his brother) to social acquaintances ('Some Ladies'), and from would-be writers like Mathew to more established figures like Hunt and Haydon, suggest that an audience of immediate friends and practising artists, occupying a specific socio-literary position, already exists. The sonnets, 'Happy is England', that to the Polish patriot, Kosciusko, and 'To Hope', like the sonnet celebrating Hunt's release from prison, proclaim a patriotic but liberal political stance. The vignette profile of Spenser on the title page, and the two epigraphs from Spenser and William Browne,[12] announce an allegiance to the great age of Elizabethan poetry, and the dedicatory sonnet expresses a nostalgia for the contemporary world's loss of the classical gods. The effect is an implicit rejection of most modern poetic taste, and an assertion that a purer and simpler vein of poetry is needed.

Keats's main preoccupations in the volume are the nature of poetry and myth. Equally insistent is the question of whether he was or was not a poet. That necessarily involved an assessment of the achievements of modern poetry, and his own possible role in its development. Keats believed himself to be living in a period of major artistic and literary recrudescence. The heroes singled out in *Sleep and Poetry*, printed as the final piece in *Poems* (1817), are Wordsworth and the Lake School, Haydon, and, of course, Hunt. In addition, Chatterton and Kirke-White (the 'lone spirits' of line 218) whose promise was 'neglected by the age' and so destroyed, are included in the modern pantheon.[13] The rejection of Pope's Augustanism and the eighteenth-century couplet is total. *Sleep and Poetry* describes the Augustans as a 'schism / Nurtured by foppery and barbarism' perverting the nature of poetry:

> . . . with a puling infant's force
> They swayed about upon a rocking horse,
> And thought it Pegasus. Ah, dismal souled!
>
> (lines 185–7)

They had disavowed Spenser, the great Elizabethans, and Milton: modern poetry had to recover the nobility and force of the 'fervid choir'. The modern poet ought also to seek inspiration from, and thus continuity with, the simplicity of the classical mythological poetry, and with the medieval poets – Petrarch and Chaucer. For Keats the times were propitious.

> . . . sweet music has been heard
> In many places – some has been upstirred
> From out its crystal dwelling in a lake,
> By a swan's ebon bill [Wordsworth's!]; from a thick brake,
> Nested and quiet in a valley mild,
> Bubbles a pipe [Hunt's] – fine sounds are floating wild
> About the earth. (lines 223–9)

Despite the inapposite symbol for Wordsworth, Keats's sense of change is evident enough. Nevertheless, he was concerned by what he saw as dangerous symptoms:

> These things are doubtless: yet in truth we've had
> Strange thunders from the potency of song;
> Mingled indeed with what is sweet and strong,
> From majesty: but in clear truth the themes
> Are ugly clubs, the poets Polyphemes
> Disturbing the grand sea. (lines 230–5)

Keats's allegorical manner leads to obscurity, which was perhaps as well at the time. His friend Woodhouse explained these lines by identifying the 'strange thunders from the potency of song' as an 'Allusion to Lord Byron, and the terrific style of poetry – to Christabel by Coleridge, &c'. Woodhouse continued:

25

The poets, says Keats, are giants like Polyphemus and his brethren, of superhuman strength, but like the eyeless Polyphemus without ability to direct their energy fitly, so that their clubs (the themes they write on . . .) only succeed in disturbing the grand sea (of poetry? or life?).[14]

A sign of Keats's obscurity here, even to knowledgeable friends, is that Hunt took the attack to be on the Lake Poets. Keats felt modern poetry was being endangered by 'themes' which were inappropriate to the truest poetry:

> But strength alone, though of the Muses born,
> Is like a fallen angel . . .
> . . . for it feeds upon the burrs,
> And thorns of life; forgetting the great end
> Of Poesy, that it should be a friend
> To soothe the cares, and lift the thoughts of man.

> (lines 241–7)

The task of Keats and his generation of poets, then, will be to ensure that poetry avoids the wrong kind of power, and to restore the 'heart-easing' role of poetry:

> And they shall be accounted poet kings
> Who simply tell the most heart-easing things.

> (lines 267–8)

Keats's youthful vision of poetry as a beneficial hallucinogenic experience, his strictures on older contemporaries, and his reading of English literary history owes too much to Hunt and too little to any comprehensive programme of reading and thinking on his own part. He also shared Hunt's sense of loss faced with the apparent obsolescence of mythology in a rationalist age. 'Glory and loveliness have passed away', 'No wreathed incense' or 'crowd of nymphs' now adorn 'The shrine of Flora in her early May', and 'Pan is no longer sought'.[15] In a complex and sophisticated modern age the simple sensuous beauty of pagan mythology can no longer function. The belief, however unhistorical, that the classical, and in particular, the ancient Greek, world was simpler, more natural, and more beautiful than the modern world was a common one. It was an impulse which encouraged unconscious pastiche. But the mature Keats is remarkable in reconciling a literalness of belief in the imaginative truth offered by Greek myths with a sense of the difficulties in taking over vehicles from another culture.

26

For a young nineteenth-century poet who was, like Keats, an admirer of Wordsworth ('He of the cloud, the cataract, the lake, / Who on Helvellyn's summit, wide awake, / Catches his freshness from archangel's wing'),[16] there was a deep anomaly in embracing classical mythology. When Hazlitt lectured on Wordsworth in 1818, he argued that the Lake Poets' commitment to the 'natural and new' was a revolution in poetry comparable to the 'principles and events of the French Revolution':

Nothing that was established was to be tolerated. All the common-place figures of poetry, tropes, allegories, personifications, with the whole heathen mythology, were instantly discarded; a classical allusion was considered as a piece of antiquated foppery.

Their notion of poetry, he continues, was founded on 'a principle of sheer humanity, on pure nature void of art'.[17] Indeed, Wordsworth himself voiced regret for the displacement of classical mythology. 'The world is too much with us', first published in 1807, ends:

> For this, for everything, we are out of tune;
> It moves us not. − Great God! I'd rather be
> A Pagan suckled in a creed outworn;
> So might I, standing on this pleasant lea,
> Have glimpses that would make me less forlorn;
> Have sight of Proteus rising from the sea;
> Or hear old Triton blow his wreathèd horn.[18]

The whole point for Wordsworth is that these visions are *not* available to him. That his final line is a clear echo of Spenser's *Colin Clouts Come Home Againe* (line 245) only underlines the unavailability of the 'outworn creed' for the modern poet.

Wordsworth's own account of the origins of myth in *The Excursion* (1814), a passage of profound importance to Keats, was firmly rational, seeing classical mythology as the outcome of pagan animism. The imagination of ancient man worked on his natural surroundings: hence the myth of Diana the huntress was created when

> The nightly Hunter, lifting up his eyes
> Towards the crescent Moon, with grateful heart
> Called on the lovely wanderer who bestowed
> That timely light, to share his joyous sport;
> And hence, a beaming Goddess with her Nymphs,
> Across the lawn and through the darksome grove . . .

Swept in the storm of chase, as Moon and Stars
Glance rapidly along the clouded heavens
When winds are blowing strong.[19]

Spirits of place were invented in gratitude:

The Traveller slaked
His thirst from Rill or gushing Fount, and thanked
The Naiad.[20]

Wordsworth's historicist analysis reduced the classical myths to a set of pleasing, but primitive, anthropomorphic stories which had led to the polytheistic religion of the Greeks. Wordsworth's and Coleridge's radical restructuring of the premises of poetry inevitably led to the problem of reconciling subjective perception to objective reality: the urgency of that gap left no room for inherited fictions, which were by then, they believed, merely poetic and without any religious assent. A corollary of that denial was to deprive the poet of the resources of narrative drawn from earlier mythologies. Truth lay in the perception of metaphysical and imaginative orders of knowing drawn directly from the poet's observation of nature and man, and these truths were to be established through symbol or in the prosaic stories of contemporary life ('The Idiot Boy' or 'Michael').

Keats and Shelley as second-generation romantics both felt an urgent need to rehabilitate Greek mythology in English poetry. Shelley's knowledge of Greek allowed him direct recourse to the originals, and this, coupled with his fierce intellectual energy, gives his ideas on myth a substantiality denied the earlier Keats. Keats's route was circuitous. Lemprière's *Classical Dictionary* along with other guides to mythology such as Spence's *Polymetis*, Hunt's example, Elizabethan translations, and Spenser's poetry provided his imaginative material. In particular, Spenser's example gave a precedent for naturalising classical deities within an English (and Irish) landscape, while Spenser's neo-Platonism fuelled Keats's belief in the truth of the imagination. Read from a 'Cockney' perspective, Spenser seemed to validate Keats's striving to reach beyond the limitations of the world he inhabited. In *Colin Clouts Come Home Againe*, the narrator describes Cynthia's virtues:

Her thoughts are like the fume of Franckincence,
Which from a golden Censer forth doth rise:

> And throwing forth sweet odours mounts fro thence
> In rolling globes vp to the vauted skies.
> There she beholds with high aspiring thought,
> The cradle of her owne creation:
> Emongst the seats of Angels heauenly wrought,
> Much like an Angell in all forme and fashion.

> (lines 608–15)

Keats's 'high aspiring thoughts' in *Poems* (1817) persistently seek, mostly ineffectively, to create the heavenly 'cradle of its own creation'. Wordsworth's reductively rational views on myth presented a radical challenge. Keats was caught between his admiration of the power and authority of Wordsworth, and his own longing for what Hazlitt called the 'dreams of art', without being able to substantiate in any satisfactory way the relation between those dreams and the reality so firmly insisted upon by one half of Wordsworth's genius.

The youthful fancies which Keats shared with G. F. Mathew point then, as they did not for Mathew, to something beyond fashionable poeticising. As a whole *Poems* (1817) embodies a consistent, if not always clearly expressed, set of beliefs about the relations between nature, imagination, and myth. The volume repeatedly asserts that the poet's imagination creates mysterious visions from natural sights, and that this is how poetry 'etherialises' the actual. Poetry's function was 'the looking upon the Sun the Moon the Stars, the Earth and its contents as materials to form greater things – that is to say etherial things' (*Letters*, i. 143). A poet looking at clouds and sheet-lightning in the western skies sees more than an ordinary person would:

> A sudden glow comes on them, naught they see
> In water, earth, or air, but poesy.
> . . . when a Poet is in such a trance,
> In air he sees white coursers paw, and prance,
> Bestridden of gay knights, in gay apparel,
> Who at each other tilt in playful quarrel,
> And what we, ignorantly, sheet-lightning call,
> Is the swift opening of their wide portal,
> When the bright warder blows his trumpet clear,
> Whose tones reach naught on earth but Poet's ear.

The 'Poet's eye' can penetrate the 'golden halls', with their festivals at which 'ladies fair' drink from goblets, while further back their 'bowers' can be 'dimly seen',

29

Of which no mortal eye can reach the flowers –
And 'tis right just, for well Apollo knows
'Twould make the Poet quarrel with the rose.

('To My Brother George', lines 21–46)

Apollo's realm of poetry is beyond the limits of human space and time and 'from all sorrowing far, far away' (line 20).

Faced with a similar sight, Wordsworth's response is quite different. In the sonnet, 'Composed after a Journey across the Hambleton Hills, in Yorkshire', written in 1802, Wordsworth describes the shapes suggested by the clouds in a western sky:

> . . . there stood Indian citadel,
> Temple of Greece, and minster with its tower
> Substantially expressed – a place for bell
> Or clock to toll from! Many a tempting isle,
> With groves that never were imagined, lay
> 'Mid seas how stedfast! objects all for the eye
> Of silent rapture; but we felt the while
> We should forget them; they are of the sky,
> And from our earthly memory fade away.[21]

Wordsworth, while admitting 'silent rapture', rejects the moment as one belonging to the Fancy. Keats attempts to move in exactly the opposite direction, towards the empyreal and etherial, yet it is striking that the preferred word for the poetic faculty in his poetry is 'Fancy' or 'Poesy' rather than 'Imagination' or 'Poetry'. The preference is a tacit admission of the problematic nature of poetry's claim to truth.

Poems (1817) is ordered so that the claims for the ability of the poetic imagination to reach towards myth through natural objects is placed in the foreground.[22] It is an implicit reply to Wordsworth. *I Stood Tip-toe*, the opening poem, begins by showing the modern poet gathering poetic 'luxuries' from nature, but quickly moves to an explanation of how classical myths came into being. The explanation echoes the rationalistic account which Keats found in Wordsworth and other contemporary sources. That is, primitive man, awed by the beauty of nature, invented stories attached to particular places.

> What first inspired a bard of old to sing
> Narcissus pining o'er the untainted spring?
> In some delicious ramble, he had found
> A little space, with boughs all woven round;

30

> And in the midst of all, a clearer pool
> Than e'er reflected in its pleasant cool
> The blue sky here and there serenely peeping
> Through tendril wreaths fantastically creeping.
> And on the bank a lonely flower he spied,
> A meek and forlorn flower, with naught of pride,
> Drooping its beauty o'er the watery clearness,
> To woo its own sad image into nearness:
> Deaf to light Zephyrus it would not move;
> But still would seem to droop, to pine, to love.
> So while the Poet stood in this sweet spot,
> Some fainter gleamings o'er his fancy shot;
> Nor was it long ere he had told the tale
> Of young Narcissus, and sad Echo's bale.
>
> (*I Stood Tip-toe*, lines 163–80)

The bulk of the poem is made up of similar accounts of the invention of the myths of Psyche and Eros, Syrinx and Pan, and that
of Endymion and Diana, but while the explanation has a superficial resemblance to Wordsworth's, *I Stood Tip-toe* puts forward a
different argument. It claims that poets enter mysterious regions
where they see 'Shapes from the invisible world' and hear 'unearthly singing / From out the middle air', bursting 'our mortal bars'
(lines 181–92). Here, as later in *Endymion*, Keats seems to imagine
the store of classical myths as existing permanently in a heavenly
version of the collective unconscious. His analysis differs from
Wordsworth's in asserting the possibility that these stories have a
persisting truth, that they are still (perhaps) available to the
modern poet, and that they are a product of the irrational.
There is a contradiction between the dedicatory sonnet regretting the loss of classical mythology, and the almost immediate
invocation of Apollo as if he were still a potent god. Marigolds
should

> Dry up the moisture from your golden lids,
> For great Apollo bids
> That in these days your praises should be sung
> On many harps, which he has lately strung.
>
> (*I Stood Tip-toe*, lines 49–52)

Apollo, god of the sun and poetry, invoked here and in *Sleep and
Poetry* as the defender and inspirer of true poets, may, mysteri-
ously, be able to function in modern times. Keats's homage to
Apollo is constant throughout his career.[23] Behind the self-doubts
and sense of belatedness expressed by *Poems* (1817), there is the

hope that the modern poet can reactivate classical myths, and that these myths have retained their ancient power to comfort mankind. Keats's attempts to create the mythic story-telling powers of the poet in an alien modern world dominate one side of his poetic search for identity.

Yet Keats's persistent search for transcendence in this early poetry is constantly threatened by uncertainty. The courage is willed. After the vision of the charioteer of poetry in *Sleep and Poetry* Keats's conviction suddenly collapses:

> The visions all are fled – the car is fled
> Into the light of heaven, and in their stead
> A sense of real things comes doubly strong,
> And, like a muddy stream, would bear along
> My soul to nothingness: but I will strive
> Against all doubtings, and will keep alive
> The thought of that same chariot . . .   (lines 155–61)

If the uncomfortable intrusion of this fear explodes much of the posturing bravura of *Poems* (1817), it also marks the fundamental honesty which, in the letters and the poems, enabled Keats to transform 'Cockney vulgarity' into a searching critique of the powers and limits of poetry.

When Keats's career is looked at from the viewpoint of *Poems* (1817), it is clear that three main areas of literature stimulated his imagination. (It is also clear that his development depends upon a repeated reworking of earlier themes and issues.) Greek mythology gave the material and the challenge for the pastoral narrative of *Endymion* and the two attempts at the Hyperion story: it also inspires *Lamia* and 'Ode on a Grecian Urn'. The medieval world of chivalry, which leads to some of the worst moments in Keats's first volume ('Calidore', 'Specimen of an Induction to a Poem'), provided the matrix out of which came *The Eve of St Agnes*, *Isabella* and 'La Belle Dame sans Merci', even though Keats's medievalism is highly eclectic, drawing less on Chaucer than on Italian examples, Spenser, Chatterton, late eighteenth-century Gothic elements from Mrs Radcliffe's novels, and the 'medieval' poems of Coleridge. Both these areas are bound up with attempts at narrative. The third main area celebrated is that of the lyric outburst in the Elizabethan period, where the most important influence is Spenser.

Keats regarded all three periods as self-sustaining worlds, on the other side of a divide from his own period, yet ones with which he believed modern poetry must re-establish continuity. Two further sources of imaginative excitement for *Poems* (1817) are fine art, particularly mythological sculpture and painting (see the end of *Sleep and Poetry*), and nature, the latter something more easily perceived by contemporary reviewers than by later readers.

Self-consciousness and ambition are constantly to the fore in Keats's first volume, but the basic patterns of thinking move in two somewhat different directions. The movement towards myth is met by one towards an analogical and non-rational mode, eschewing narrative. The choice between a poetry of myth and a poetry of symbol is already apparent in *Poems*. Myth involved telling a story which carried an overall meaning. It forced Keats towards an explicitness at odds with the intuitive and sceptical side of his poetic sensibility.

Keats came to realise, as he said to Reynolds early in 1818, 'We hate poetry that has a palpable design upon us – and if we do not agree, seems to put its hand in its breeches pocket' (*Letters*, i. 224). Poetry of any kind should be 'great & unobtrusive': discursive thought ('consequitive reasoning') disturbed poetry, which ought to intuit meaning through sensation and imagery. Even in the early poetry a sudden coalescence of sensation and association leads to intimations, momentary recognitions, of another order of truth. The sonnet, 'After dark vapours have oppressed our plains', was written after *Poems* (1817) had been made ready for the press. Although its last phrase sentimentally invites the reader to brood on the luxury of a 'Poet's death', the closing catalogue is unassertively direct:

> And calmest thoughts come round us – as of leaves
>   Budding – fruit ripening in stillness – autumn suns
> Smiling at eve upon the quiet sheaves –
> Sweet Sappho's cheek – a sleeping infant's breath –
>   The gradual sand that through an hour-glass runs –
> A woodland rivulet – a Poet's death.

Most of this is unforced. The 'calmest thoughts' are in fact images. It is their connections, of completions and beginnings, which invite the reader to see them adding up to an overall 'meaning'.[24]

The technique, identical in principle to that in *I Stood Tip-toe* or much of *Sleep and Poetry*, but without the paraphernalia of forced 'significance' and slippery allegorising, prefigures the symbolic manner of the later Keats, where, as in a central body of twentieth-century poetry, meaning is taken up into the image. The 'autumn suns / Smiling at eve upon the quiet sheaves' looks forward to the fullness of consolatory celebration of 'To Autumn' whose final catalogue defies paraphrase, just as the conclusion to Coleridge's 'Frost at Midnight' contains the poem's meaning within the mysterious reciprocity of light between the icicles and the moon:

> . . . the secret ministry of frost
> Shall hang them up in silent icicles,
> Quietly shining to the quiet Moon.

Similarly, a direct line connects the 'pigeon tumbling in clear summer air' in *Sleep and Poetry* (line 93) with the 'gathering swallows' which twitter in the skies of 'To Autumn', but also with the ending of Wallace Stevens's 'Sunday Morning':

> And, in the isolation of the sky,
> At evening, casual flocks of pigeons make
> Ambiguous undulations as they sink,
> Downward to darkness, on extended wings.

3

Endymion: 'Pretty Paganism' and 'Purgatory Blind'

Endymion: A Poetic Romance (1818), started shortly after the publication of Keats's first volume, is a 'dream of poetry', of youth and of love, yeasty, ardent and diffuse. Almost before its completion Keats dismissed his pastoral as an adolescent failure, though he also knew that its 4,000 lines of poetry had been essential to his development as a poet. Looking back on its composition, he wrote to his publisher,

> In Endymion, I leaped headlong into the Sea, and thereby have become better acquainted with the Soundings, the quicksands, & the rocks, than if I had stayed upon the green shore, and piped a silly pipe, and took tea & comfortable advice. (*Letters*, i. 374)

As this suggests, *Endymion* is more a poem in process than a considered whole. Keats takes up again the story of the love of the moon-goddess, Diana, for the shepherd-prince, Endymion, with which he had concluded *I Stood Tip-toe*.

Endymion is a Romantic quest-poem portraying the poet's search for true imaginative powers. Its structure follows the progressive tests and initiation-rites through which the hero proves himself. Most of Endymion's confusions in the poem arise from Diana's decision to visit the poet-prince first in the form of an unknown goddess, and later in guise of an Indian Maid. In love with all three, Endymion's bewildered and divided feelings are resolved by the long-delayed discovery that all three are one. The poem concludes with the immortalisation of Endymion and his marriage to Diana.

Endymion's plot is an argument for the essential interconnectedness of human love and the truth of ideal beauty. If Endymion longs for his goddess, Diana pursues her union with an earthly lover with equal determination. The poem's broad outline is clear enough. In Book I, the hero is set apart from his Latmian subjects by the 'cankering venom' (I. 396) caused by his dream of a heavenly goddess, which threatens his worship of the moon

(Diana), and has left him dissatisfied with reality. Endymion is the alienated modern poet bearing the cost of consciousness. To attain his dream of ideal love, Endymion is initiated first into the mysteries of the heavens (Book I), then into those of the earth (Book II) and those of the sea (Book III). In the final book, he is returned to earth. The appearance of the Indian Maid, with whom Endymion instantly falls in love, forces him to choose between actual human love and his dreams. His choice of human love is, ironically, the last test in his progress to godhead.

Endymion also shows its hero progressively learning to sympathise with the sufferings of other lovers, as the stories of Alpheus and Arethusa (II. 932–1017) and of Glaucus (III. 187–1015) are meant to show. In addition to knowledge of the universe, empathy with human pain, and a final commitment to earthly life, are essential to Endymion's simultaneous assumption of poethood and godhead. However, interpretations of the allegory are so various[1] that, for most readers, *Endymion* offers the sort of pleasure which Keats attributed to the long poem:

> Do not the Lovers of Poetry like to have a little Region to wander in where they may pick and choose, and in which the images are so numerous that many are forgotten and found new in a second Reading: which may be food for a Week's stroll in the Summer? (*Letters*, i. 170)

Endymion's 'poetic romance' is the first sustained example of Keats's style and highly personal use of mythology, artificial and yet true to feeling. Both John Bayley and Christoper Ricks reject the common judgement (Keats's own) on *Endymion*'s immaturity: 'the central Keats is the rich poet of *Endymion* and "The Eve of St Agnes" rather than the sombre mature poet (strained and against the grain) of, say, *The Fall of Hyperion*. Keats's art at its best risks vulgarity: "It turns what might appear mean and embarrassing into what is rich and *disconcerting*." '[2]

The rejection here of *The Fall of Hyperion* seems to me mistaken and the case for *Endymion* over-stated, but the up-ending of conventional judgement is salutary. At issue is the verbal excesses which have embarrassed earlier and later critics, yet *Endymion* is most alive when real feelings invest its mythological figures with disconcerting vitality. Both Ricks and Bayley cite the description of Niobe:

> . . . Perhaps, the trembling knee
> And frantic gape of lonely Niobe –
> Poor, lonely Niobe! – when her lovely young

> Were dead and gone, and her caressing tongue
> Lay a lost thing upon her paly lip,
> And very, very deadliness did nip
> Her motherly cheeks.   (I. 337–43)

Bayley points to the potency of 'gape', and says,

This is the real anguish of the human heart . . . The contrast between *caressing*, with its firm sexual meaning, and the terrible disregard for itself of this face in torment, would be almost too painful were it not that the intensity of the image 'causes all disagreeables to evaporate.'[3]

In extreme grief, the human face becomes inhumanly distorted, wholly unconscious of how it might appear to others.[4] The threat which 'gape' poses to poetic decorum reflects the undecorous nature of grief. While the lines allow the reader to feel the physical and emotional intensity of Niobe's grief, they respect its otherness. There is no prying into or savouring of Niobe's grief: it is registered through feeling and sensation but with objectivity.

John Hamilton Reynolds was alone among contemporary critics in recognising the lack of Romantic 'egotism' in *Endymion*'s treatment of natural scenes – 'You do not see him, when you see her [Nature]'.[5] As in 'To Autumn', while humanising the natural world, Keats celebrates its non-human life. In the 'Hymn to Pan' he writes,

> O thou, to whom
> Broad-leaved fig trees even now foredoom
> Their ripen'd fruitage; yellow-girted bees
> Their golden honeycombs; our village leas
> Their fairest-blossomed beans and poppied corn . . .
>   (I. 251–5)

The closed fullness of natural 'completions' (line 260), of living things fulfilling their functions with the yearly cycle, is mediated directly to the reader.

Keats's sense of the differing life of other ways of being gives vitality to his recreation of mythological figures, as in his description of Cybele:

> . . . alone – alone –
> In sombre chariot; dark foldings thrown
> About her majesty, and front death-pale,
> With turrets crowned. Four maned lions hale
> The sluggish wheels; solemn their toothed maws,

> Their surly eyes brow-hidden, heavy paws
> Uplifted drowsily, and nervy tails
> Cowering their tawny brushes. (II. 640–7)

On other occasions, his gods take on the scale and grandeur he saw in sculpture and mythological paintings:

> Like old Deucalion mountained o'er the flood,
> Or blind Orion hungry for the morn. (II. 197–8)

The first part of Book I offers sustained passages recreating *Endymion*'s lost pagan world. The early morning gathering of the forest population round Pan's altar (lines 89–231) and the ensuing stanzaic hymn to Pan (lines 232–306) evoke the simplicity and physical beauty of the pagan world with an animist sense of awe. The pastoral world created has a physical actuality touched by a sense of poignancy at its irrevocable loss. Keats's source is not Greek literature itself, but an amalgamation from second-hand sources. Similarly eclectic and similarly successful are the descriptions of the triumphal progress of Bacchus (IV. 193–272) and that of Circe's route (III. 490–537).

The extreme harshness with which Keats rejected his romance ('every error denoting a feverish attempt, rather than a deed accomplished') was in direct proportion to his fervent belief in the importance and fragility of the world which *Endymion* attempted to recall. 'I hope I have not in too late a day touched the beautiful mythology of Greece, and dulled its brightness.'[6] The endeavour to recreate 'the beautiful mythology of Greece' lies at the centre of any understanding of what Keats was trying to do in *Endymion*. Although the poem attempts too many things at once, its themes and argument call for attention as much as its style.

Wordsworth's dismissal of the Homeric hymn to Pan as 'a Very pretty piece of Paganism'[7] attacked Keats's ambitious venture precisely at the point which caused the young poet most anxiety – the fear that *Endymion*'s failure desecrated the grand simplicity and beauty of the Greek world, reducing it to mere decoration. For both Keats and Wordsworth, the poem's paganism was an important matter. The painter, Benjamin Haydon, ascribed Wordsworth's reaction to the fact that his 'puling Christian feelings were annoyed'.[8]

Endymion is a serious effort to imagine the 'natural theology' of its 'Greek' world. Keats shared Hunt's dislike of institutionalised Christianity, parsons, and the Christian belief in man's innate corruption, but, as an unassertive agnostic, held well short of

Shelley's avowed atheism. Sympathising with Benjamin Bailey, who had been disappointed in his hopes of a curacy, Keats told his Anglican friend that there were two sources of consolation for the troubles of this world, those 'of Religion and [those of] undepraved Sensations. of the Beautiful. the poetical in all things.'[9] For Keats, Joseph Severn reported, the essence of the Greek spirit was 'the Religion of the Beautiful, the Religion of Joy, as he used to call it'.[10] *Endymion*'s opening lines, beginning 'A thing of beauty is a joy for ever', assert that the 'sweet dreams' of art, 'Some shape of beauty' can move away 'the pall / From our dark spirits' (I. 1–13).

The danger that a modern poet's reworking of Greek myth might lead only to insipid prettification was, as some of Hunt's poetry showed, real enough. But the Hellenic revival of these years could cut deeper. *Endymion*'s 'religion' and its ideas on the nature and origin of myths are best understood when Keats's response to mythological paintings is taken in conjunction with contemporary accounts of the origins of Greek mythology. Keats owned a copy of William Godwin's *The Pantheon: or Ancient History of the Gods of Greece and Rome . . .* (1806), a book aimed at the young reader and published under the name of 'Edward Baldwin'. Godwin writes:

The most important senses of the human body are seeing and hearing . . . it is a delightful thing to take a walk in fields, and look at the skies and trees and the corn-fields and the waving grass, to observe the mountains and the lakes and the rivers and the seas, to smell the new-mown hay, to inhale the fresh and balmy breeze, and to hear the wild warblings of the birds: but a man does not enjoy these in their most perfect degree, till his imagination becomes a little visionary; the human mind does not have a landscape without life and without a soul: we are delighted to talk to the objects around us, and to feel as if they understood and sympathised with us: we create, by the power of fancy, a human form and a human voice in those scenes, which to a man of literal understanding may appear dead and lifeless.[11]

Hence, according to Godwin, Greek religion 'gave animation and life to all existence: it had its Naiads, Gods of the rivers, its Tritons and Nereids, Gods of the seas, its Satyrs, Fauns and Dryads, Gods of the woods and trees, and its Boreas, Euros, Auster and Zephyr, Gods of the winds.'[12] If this admiration for the simplicity and the sensuousness of the ancient Greek world is linked to the way in which Keats and his immediate circle looked at painters' representations of mythological episodes, the kind of effects he was aiming at in *Endymion* becomes clearer. Mythological paintings made the vitality of Greek myth live again for the modern viewer. In looking at a painting, Hazlitt wrote,

We are abstracted to another sphere: we breathe empyrean air; we enter into the minds of Raphael, of Titian, of Poussin, of the Caracci, and look at nature with their eyes; we live in time past, and seem identified with the permanent form of things . . . Here is the mind's true home. The contemplation of truth and beauty is the proper object for which we were created, which calls forth the most intense desires of the soul, and of which it never tires.[13]

The 'permanent form of things' are perceived not through a Wordsworthian meditation upon nature, but through the 'abstractions' of an art work. *Endymion*'s mythological figures and inset stories are vehicles for Keats's exploration of beauty and truth, and an attempt to recreate, as Poussin and Titian had in painting, the 'beautiful mythology' the Greeks had drawn from nature. For Keats there were dangers in the analogy between poetry and painting. Kenneth Burke has said that 'the form of thought in Keats is mystical, in terms of an *eternal present*'.[14] The 'eternal present' of a painting's arrested time is hard to imitate in poetry, particularly in a narrative poem. To take one from many examples, the Bower of Adonis episode (II. 387–427), which draws on Poussin's *Echo and Narcissus*,[15] comes close to halting the story's progress. The pull between narrative and Keats's predilection for static 'pictures' is an important cause of the reader's difficulties in following *Endymion*. Nevertheless, the way in which Keats and Hazlitt saw Poussin, Claude, Titian, and Raphael points to the nobility of conception which underlies the romance. The 'mind's true home' is not in the imperfections of contemporary society, but in 'another sphere' in which the soul can contemplate truth and beauty. Mythological paintings demonstrate how a modern recreation of ancient stories can seem to create an alternative timeless world.

Endymion is less an act of historical imagination (though it is that), than an imaginative vision of the past which implicitly offers a principle in answer to contemporary despair and despondency. It may, indeed, be in part a reply to the apparent pessimism of Shelley's *Alastor, or the Spirit of Solitude* (1816).[16] Since the 'gloom' of the second generation Romantics was fuelled by a shared anger at the political and social repression of the times coupled with their knowledge of the failure of the French Revolution, *Endymion*'s mythological 'Greece' proposes an alternative to the dominant values and beliefs represented by the repressive policies of Castlereagh and Sidmouth, and the narrow puritanical values of the Society for the Propagation of Christian Knowledge. The shrill and obscure attack upon the 'baaing vanities' of bishops, kings, and emperors at the beginning of Book III (lines 1–22) was intended by Keats not just as an attack upon reactionary regimes in general, but as a specific attack upon 'the present Ministry'.[17] *Endymion* is a rejection of the unheroic and oppressive values of the rulers of Regency Britain.

What is placed against their tyranny, however, is not a political answer, but an assertion of the primacy of other values. While *Endymion* is not explicitly anti-Christian (and was extravagantly admired by a dedicated Christian like Haydon), the whole drift of the poem is to place humanity and human love at its centre. The animist worship of Pan in Book I, the belief in a 'Great Maker', and the shepherd-king's ascent to godhead, imagine a pattern of belief which ignores the doctrines of the Trinity and Original Sin in favour of a theistic natural religion. It is a religion which believes in an after-life and the immortality of the individual human soul, and which regards human love, both in its physical and spiritual manifestations, as generative and self-transcending. A passage towards the end of the poem denies the virtues of self-denial and chastity. It occurs after Endymion has chosen the Indian Maid in preference to his dream. He is then told that there is a ban upon their love: Endymion plans to take up his kingly duties, but dedicates himself to the solitary life of a hermit, worshipping Diana. Unaware that he has just succeeded in his ultimate trial, Endymion breaks out bitterly against his enforced solitude:

> 'And by old Rhadamanthus' tongue of doom,
> This *dusk religion, pomp of solitude,*
> And the Promethean clay by thief endued,
> By old Saturnus' forelock, by his head
> Shook with eternal palsy, I did wed
> Myself to *things of light* from infancy;
> And thus to be cast out, thus lorn to die,
> Is sure enough to make a mortal man
> Grow impious.'   (IV. 953–61; my italics)

The impiety is justified. Self-denial, chastity and gloom are unnecessary since the Maid and Diana are one. Love and fulfilment are the natural order. Endymion's dedication to 'things of light' triumphs over the 'dusk religion' of solitary worship. The classical allusions, although obscure, probably identify the 'dusk religion' with Christianity's suspicion of sensual love, and the stigma cast on human sexuality by the story of Adam and Eve.[18] The poem's conclusion, then, 'proves' the truth of Endymion's discovery in Book I – 'this earthly love has power to make / Men's being mortal, immortal' (lines 843–4). Although subversive of conventional belief, *Endymion* is not an argument for free love.

Its conclusion circles back to and explains the opening invocation. The claim, 'A thing of beauty is a joy for ever', does not advocate a life-denying aestheticism. Rather, the knowledge of beauty 'binds' us to the earth:

> Therefore, on every morrow, are we wreathing
> A flowery band to bind us to the earth,
> Spite of despondence, of the inhuman dearth
> Of noble natures, of the gloomy days,
> Of all the unhealthy and o'er-darkened ways
> Make for our searching: yes, in spite of all,
> Some shape of beauty moves away the pall
> From our dark spirits. Such the *sun*, the *moon*,
> *Trees* old, and young . . .
> And such too is the grandeur of the dooms
> We have imagined for the *mighty dead*;
> All *lovely tales* that we have heard or read –
> An endless fountain of immortal drink,
> Pouring unto us from the heaven's brink.
>
> (I. 6–24: my italics)

We are bound to earth, despite its evils and shortcomings, by the human imagination's 'searching' of the natural world, its memory of the 'mighty dead', and its access to earlier poetry. Throughout *Endymion*, Keats sees the role of the poet in the same terms as he had in *I Stood Tip-toe*. The truths contained in the natural world remain immanent until an individual human imagination makes them apprehensible through poetry. Once created, the story is given its 'universal freedom', and its truths are available to later readers (II. 829–41). It is the insistence upon the necessity of human intervention which makes Keats's 'Platonism' highly idiosyncratic. Refusing the normal Platonic ascent from sensual to ideal love, *Endymion* says that the ideal is only apprehended through individual sensual experience, and through a commitment to the actual. But the individual imagination's discovery of divine truth from the materials of the world comes very close to claiming that man creates his own immortality. The point is made explicitly, if briefly, in Book I. When human beings combine and 'interknit' with love, says Endymion,

> Life's self is nourished by its proper pith,
> And we are nurtured like a pelican brood.
>
> (lines 814–5)

This is not the usual position taken in *Endymion*, which normally says that human imaginings are drawn from an eternal source, but the lines stress that the imagination be grounded upon human actuality. *Endymion*'s overall pattern is an optimistic one. The re-imagining of an ancient Greek myth leads to the creation of a modern myth, pointing the way to the possible fulfilment of humanity's potential, a potential denied by the dominant political and religious beliefs of the day.

Keats's use of Greek mythology for these purposes was not unusual. From the Enlightenment onwards sceptical thinkers from Voltaire to Hume had used pre-Christian mythology to question Christianity's claims to unique truth. As Marilyn Butler points out, in the second decade of the nineteenth century Greek mythology provided writers like Hunt, Peacock, Hazlitt, Keats, and Shelley, with an important occasion for dissent (whether liberal, deist, radical, or atheist) from prevailing orthodoxies.[19] Keats, like Hazlitt, saw the Greek world as one which attested to the pre-eminence of Art and 'Beauty'. *Endymion* adds to that a metaphoric equation between human love and poetry. The four books of *Endymion* are a prolonged speculative attempt to establish an equivalence between sexual love and poetry's ability to link the mortal and immortal spheres.

The poem's allegory wishes to force this analogy into an identity, hence the insistently physical depiction of heavenly loving throughout the poem, which risks both obscurity and ridicule. However, the questions forced upon him in the course of composition were, from autumn 1817 onwards, increasingly taken up in the letters. There his 'speculations' are more easily understood. Keats's important letter on the nature of the imagination, written to Bailey on 22 November 1817, outlines the intended centre of *Endymion*. He is replying to Bailey's 'momentary start [i.e., fears about] the authenticity of the Imagination':

I am certain of nothing but of the holiness of the Heart's affections and the truth of Imagination – What the imagination seizes as Beauty must be truth – whether it existed before or not – for I have the same Idea of all our Passions as of Love they are all in their sublime, creative of essential Beauty. (*Letters*, i. 184)

Keats continues his letter to Bailey by referring him to passages in *Endymion*:

In a Word, you may know my favorite Speculation by my first Book and the little song ['O Sorrow', IV. 146–81] I sent in my last [letter] – which is a representation from the fancy of the probable mode of operating in these Matters – The Imagination may be compared to Adam's dream – he awoke and found it truth. I am the more zealous in this affair, because I have never yet been able to perceive how any thing can be known for truth by consequitive reasoning – and yet it must be – Can it be that even the greatest Philosopher ever arrived at his goal without putting aside numerous objections. (*ibid.*, i. 184–5)

This is not a simple assertion that imaginative truth is superior to rational thinking. Keats makes two related points. Consequitive thinking alone cannot reach truth: in order to formulate a new concept, even the philosopher (and by implication the scientist), has to make an imaginative leap, ignoring apparently contradictory evidence. Secondly, a truth is not properly *known* until it is imaginatively comprehended. In both cases, the imagination creates truth. 'The Imagination may be compared to Adam's dream – he awoke and found it truth.'

This is a realisation central to Keats's own poetry, but goes beyond it. However, the 'speculation' which immediately follows this passage puts forward a less satisfactory belief explored by *Endymion*. The problem is caused by Keats's sceptical humanism, a humanism which nevertheless wishes to believe in the immortality of the individual soul:

O for a Life of Sensations rather than of Thoughts! It is 'a Vision in the form of Youth' a Shadow of reality to come – and this consideration has further conv[i]nced me . . . that we shall enjoy ourselves here after by having what we called happiness on Earth repeated in a finer tone and so repeated – And yet such a fate can only befall those who delight in sensation rather than hunger as you do after Truth. (*Letters*, i. 185)

Endymion believes that the imagination, working on sensation and intense human passion, prefigures a transcendent world hereafter, a world of etherealised human happiness. Keats tried to explain his belief to Bailey by asking him to remember

being surprised with an old Melody – in a delicious place – by a delicious voice . . . at the time it first operated on your soul – do you not remember forming to you[r]self the singer's face more beautiful than [written 'that'] it was possible and yet with the elevation of the Moment you did not think so – even then you were mounted on the

Wings of Imagination so high – that the Prototype must be here after
– that delicious face you will see – What a time!   (*ibid.*)

This heady mixture of Platonic idealism and youthful longing
means that *Endymion*'s 'Vision in the form of Youth' and its reality
to come are persistently imagined in terms of 'delicious faces' and
of human love 'repeated in a finer tone'. When Diana, the moon-
goddess, describes their future life in heaven to Endymion, her
mortal lover, poetry and sexuality are inextricably mingled:

> . . . Now a soft kiss –
> Ay, by that kiss, I vow an endless bliss,
> An immortality of passion's thine.
> Ere long I will exalt thee to the shine
> Of heaven ambrosial . . .
> And I will tell thee stories of the sky,
> And breathe thee whispers of its minstrelsy.
> My happy love will overwing all bounds!
> O let me melt into thee; let the sounds
> Of our close voices marry at their birth;
> Let us entwine hoveringly – O dearth
> Of human words! roughness of mortal speech!
> Lispings empyrean will I sometime teach
> Thine honeyed tongue – lute-breathings, which I gasp
> To have thee understand   (II. 806–21)

'What a time!' Tenor and vehicle are confusingly related. Is the
lover's embrace a kind of heavenly poetry, or the heavenly embrace meant as a metaphor of poetry's and the imagination's
powers to transcend the physical? In *Endymion* the answer is, quite
simply, both.

Keats's version of neo-Platonic love no doubt owes much to his
early reading of Spenser, but the literalness of his equation of
divine and earthly love is informed more by adolescent fantasy
than by any apprehension of Heavenly Love. Endymion begins
the exchange with Diana:

> O known Unknown! from whom my being sips
> Such darling essence, wherefore may I not
> Be ever in these arms? in this sweet spot
> Pillow my chin for ever? ever press
> These toying hands and kiss their smooth excess?
>   (II. 739–43)

His speech ends in over-excited metaphor:

> 'Enchantress! tell me by this soft embrace,
> By the most soft completion of thy face,

Those lips, O slippery blisses, twinkling eyes
And by these tenderest, milky sovereignties –
These tenderest – and by the nectar-wine,
The passion – (II. 756–61)

Keats's difficulties in describing women's breasts reaches an apotheosis here,[20] and the coy phrasing of these lines invites mockery. But there is also a kind of innocence, springing from Keats's idealism. The long account in Book I of the 'Pleasure Thermometer' (lines 777–842) explains *Endymion*'s metaphoric linkage between immortal poetic imaginings and physical love. It is a passage whose composition Keats felt to be 'a regular stepping of the Imagination towards a Truth',[21] and begins with an apparently Platonic assertion:

Wherein lies happiness? In that which becks
Our ready minds to fellowship divine,
A fellowship with essence; till we shine,
Full alchemized, and free of space. Behold
The clear religion of heaven!

The scale climbs from the physical enjoyment of nature, to our apprehension of poetic tales in natural settings and the pleasures of music and poetry, to 'love and friendship', culminating in 'love' which 'interknits' our souls 'so wingedly': indeed, human love may be more than the 'mere commingling of passionate breath' –

. . . but who, of men, can tell
That flowers would bloom, or that green fruit would swell
To melting pulp, that fish would have bright mail,
The earth its dower of river, wood, and vale,
The meadows runnels, runnels pebble-stones,
The seed its harvest, or the lute its tones,
Tones ravishment, or ravishment its sweet,
If human souls did never kiss and greet? (I. 835–42)

Benjamin Bailey was right to fear that *Endymion*'s imaginative stepping towards truth came close to endorsing 'that abominable principle of *Shelley's* – that *Sensual Love* is the principle of *things*.'[22] Keats does not go that far: instead he invents a sensual Platonism in which human love and poetry are linked manifestations of the same power which both give access to immortal truth.

The resultant balance between physical and ideal love is unstable. Uncertainty about the relationship between human and immortal worlds is as much a result of the intrusion of Keats's own erotic fantasies as the weak control over his allegorical narrative.

For instance, the story of Alpheus, the river-god, and the nymph Arethusa, is meant to demonstrate that by the end of Book II Endymion has taken on the powers of the original poets who invented Graeco-Roman myths. The episode (II. 914–1017) is a copy-book example of natural beauty providing the ancient poets with the source of 'lovely tales'. Endymion hears the sound of two gushing springs, and invents the story of the love of Arethusa and Alpheus which cannot be consummated because Arethusa is one of Diana's huntresses, and therefore bound to chastity. Not only does Endymion invent the story, but having done so appeals to Diana to allow their love to be assuaged, thus demonstrating the true poet's necessary sympathy with suffering. But Keats's telling of the story separates off from the allegory, becoming an 'aesthetically' distanced fantasy of an imagined sexual encounter. Arethusa is prevented from bathing in Alpheus' waters a second time: he regrets being deprived of the opportunity

> . . . to run
> In amorous rillets down her shrinking form!
> To linger on her lily shoulders, warm
> Between her kissing breasts, and every charm
> Touch raptured! – See how painfully I flow! (II. 944–8)

(In the draft version Alpheus kisses 'raptur'd' – even to her milky toes'.) It is no surprise that when Cupid is apostrophised as god of love, the etherial 'essences' of 'fellowship divine' turn out to be directly physical:

> O sweetest essence! sweetest of all minions!
> God of warm pulses, and dishevelled hair,
> And panting bosoms bare! (III. 983–5)

The earthly and ideal realms have changed places. It requires a sympathetic reader to see what Keats's allegory is trying to say in the Alpheus and Arethusa story.

Other reactions were possible. The reviewer in *The British Critic* assaulted *Endymion*'s sexual impurity:

not all the flimsy veil of words in which he would involve immoral images, can atone for their impurity; and we will not disgust our readers by retailing to them the artifices of vicious refinement, by which, under the semblance of 'slippery blisses, twinkling eyes, soft completion of faces, and smooth excess of hands', he would palm upon the unsuspicious and the innocent imaginations better adapted to the stews.[23]

The British Critic isolates the cause of Byron's violent revulsion to 'Johnny Keats's *p*[*i*]*ss a bed* poetry'.[24] In part this is a clash of sensibilities – Byron's *sang froid* when dealing with Don Juan's escapades is the antithesis of Keats's intense identification with the young lovers in *The Eve of St Agnes*. Byron's objections went beyond *Endymion*. In 1820 he wrote to his publisher, Murray, 'such writing is a sort of mental masturbation – Keats is always f[ri]gg[in]g his *Imagination*. I don't mean he is *indecent* [Byron would have been less disturbed if Keats had been], but viciously soliciting his own ideas into a state'.[25]

Byron's objections to Keats were also partly animated by class antagonism. G. M. Matthews shrewdly observes:

This sort of socio-sexual revulsion is an oddly persistent feature of Keats criticism . . . Its origin seems to lie in the disturbance created by a deep response to Keats's poetic sensuality in conflict with a strong urge towards sexual apartheid. At any rate, Byron's astonishing outbursts . . . must have had some such components. That is, it was more or less accepted – since Crabbe and Wordsworth had insisted on it – that the domestic emotions of the lower classes were a fit subject for poetry; but that a poet of the lower classes should play with *erotic* emotions was insufferable, unless these were expressed in a straightforward peasant dialect, as with Burns or Clare.[26]

If class was one cause of the anger directed at Keats's 'Cockney' temerity in portraying erotic emotions, another, and more powerful cause was that Keats's approving depiction of sexuality cut through the conventional belief that ladies had, in the words of *The British Critic*, 'unsuspicious and innocent imaginations'. While Keats's own attitude to women was frequently ambivalent, *Endymion* assumes that women as well as men have strong sexual drives. Arethusa 'burns' as a result of bathing in Alpheus' waters:

> But ever since I heedlessly did lave
> In thy deceitful stream, a panting glow
> Grew strong within me: wherefore serve me so,
> And call it love? (II. 969–72)

And throughout the pastoral it is the women who seduce the men.

From a twentieth-century viewpoint Keats may seem frequently guilty of an adolescent failure of taste. The poem now looks naive rather than shocking. However, the schizophrenic reaction to *Endymion* when it was published in 1818 ('a dream of poetry', 'better adapted to the stews'), does raise the question of what Keats and his publishers thought they were presenting to the public. Taylor worked very closely on the manuscript of *Endymion*, suggesting verbal changes and seeing it through the press on Keats's behalf: there is no sign at this stage that the man, later so exercised over the impropriety of the revised version of *The Eve of St Agnes*, saw the narrative as anything other than 'a dream of poetry' or that he doubted Keats's genius. Similarly, Keats writing to his young sister Fanny told her the story of his poem, remarking, 'I dare say [you] have read this and all the other beautiful Tales which have come down from the ancient times of that beautiful Greece. If you have not let me know and I will tell you more at large of others quite as delightful' (*Letters*, i. 154).

The violence of *The British Critic* stems precisely from a fear that the Ovidian stories, taken too literally, were not at all suitable for young ladies. Yet while the readers in the later twentieth century cannot avoid reading *Endymion* as a series of often barely disguised erotic fantasies, it was not only Keats's publisher who read the poem as an idealistic romance. Richard Woodhouse was particularly pleased to tell Keats in December 1818 that his own copy had been borrowed by Mary Frogley and then read and admired by Jane and Maria Porter 'of romance celebrity' – Jane Porter, author of *The Scottish Chief* and other works, thought the poem showed 'true Parnassian fire' (*Letters*, ii. 9–10).[27]

The response of readers like these indicates that 'romance' created a *cordon sanitaire* which allowed the expression and enjoyment of feelings and emotions which could not be consciously admitted. Sexual doings among the Greek gods were 'pretty' fictions, suitable for young ladies.[28] Keats's reaction to Woodhouse's offer to introduce him to the Misses Porter was quizzical:

I must needs feel flattered by making an impression on a set of Ladies – I should be content to do so in meretricious romance verse if they alone and not Men were to judge.   (*Letters*, i. 412)

'Meretricious romance verse' is the kind of anodyne romance which offered the pleasure of mildly titilating fantasy to an unreflecting audience. Keats may have felt that, in the end, *Endymion* had achieved no more than this, but he had hoped for readers willing to pay serious attention to the poem's substantial themes. That Taylor and Woodhouse failed to perceive the underlying subversiveness of *Endymion* is not surprising: Keats's subject matter resembles that of conventional romance (for example, Mrs Tighe's *Psyche* (1805)),[29] and its rambling allegory is sufficiently oblique to obscure its real argument. The similarity between Keats's poetry and the flaccid romances of the day was close enough for some readers to confuse one with the other.

Endymion does not succeed in establishing a properly meaningful relation between the 'etherial' and mundane. It does, however, show Keats already struggling with his major preoccupations. Throughout the poem there is a latent, sometimes open, fissure between 'the power to dream deliciously' (II. 708) and the actualities of 'dull mortality's harsh net' (III. 907). 'Beauty' is found within a dream, or even in a dream within a dream which ends abruptly in the sleep of unconsciousness (I. 553–709). But the promise that 'solitary thinkings' which dodge 'Conception to the very bourne of heaven' will leaven 'this dull and clodded earth' giving it 'a touch etherial – a new birth' (I. 293–8) proves elusive, and may be only a dream.

> There never lived a mortal man, who bent
> His appetite beyond his natural sphere,
> But starved and died. (IV. 646–8)

Throughout *Endymion* there is a persistent movement towards associating the moment of fulfilment not just with unconsciousness but with death: 'we might embrace and die: voluptuous thought!' (IV. 759). The Indian Maid's pursuit of pleasure and beauty leads to sorrow –

> Come then, Sorrow!
> Sweetest Sorrow!
> Like an own babe I nurse thee on my breast:
> I thought to leave thee
> And deceive thee,
> But now of all the world I love thee best.
>
> (IV. 279–84)

There is also a sinister aspect of love. As a whole, the Glaucus episode (III. 187–1017) symbolises the role of the poet, whose suffering and vision brings comfort to humanity, forecasting the subject of Keats's two poems on Hyperion, but his tale begins ominously. Glaucus is seduced by the enchantress Circe, but the promised 'long love-dream' (III. 440) turns to nightmare: he is the victim of the 'arbitrary queen of sense' (III. 459). Circe's rout of tormented animal shapes, who wish to 'be delivered from this cumbrous flesh, . . . this gross, detestable, filthy mesh' (III. 551–2), are clearly images of revulsion in the aftermath of sexual gratification. Circe is the principle of female sexuality as destroyer, and this passage (III. 417–614) an expression of the tensions which lie behind 'La Belle Dame sans Merci' and *Lamia*.

The initial optimism of *Endymion*'s combination of 'humanistic hedonism'[30] and aching idealism comes close to being denied by powerful undercurrents in the poem – the ambiguity of the hero's dreams and visions, his recurrent despondency and long withdrawal from kingly duties, and the threat of the real, all question the efficacy of the religion of beauty.

Keats's maturing views on poetry and the imagination could not be contained by *Endymion*, but were worked out in the 'speculations' of the letters. 'Speculation', containing the Latin sense of spying out as well as the usual abstract meaning, is Keats's own word for his exploratory forays. Their truth then is provisional: they represent a hypothesis with no claim to ultimate or exclusive truth. Indeed, 'eve[r]y point of thought is the centre of an intellectual world' and –

almost any Man may like the Spider spin from his own inwards his own airy Citadel – the points of leaves and twigs on which the Spider begins her work are few and she fills the Air with a beautiful circuiting

(*Letters*, i. 231–2)

In both his speculations and his poetry Keats's mode is essentially exploratory and tentative. He wrote to Bailey in March 1818, 'I must once for all tell you I have not one Idea of the truth of any of my speculations', and went so far as to say, 'I am sometimes so very sceptical as to think Poetry itself a mere Jack a lanthern to amuse whoever may chance to be struck with its brilliance' (*Letters*, i. 242). It is precisely the ability to hold contrary truths together in creative tension which Keats saw as the essential quality which goes

. . . to form a Man of Achievement especially in Literature & which Shakespeare posessed so enormously – I mean *Negative Capability*, that is when man is capable of being in uncertainties, Mysteries, doubts, without any irritable reaching after fact & reason – Coleridge, for instance, would let go by a fine isolated verisimilitude caught from the Penetralium of mystery, from being incapable of remaining content with half knowledge. (*Letters*, i. 193–4)

Keats's famous remark, made in December 1817 while finishing *Endymion*, is at the heart of his own achievement. The ambitions of poetry and its claims to a supra-rational and intuitive order of truth, were themselves at risk. With his suspicion that poetry may be no more than a 'Jack a lanthern', Keats entertains a peculiarly modern fear that the secrecy and inviolability of the products of the imagination may offer false consolation, may be, in the end, illusory. Even *Endymion*, committed as it is to affirming the superior truth of poetry, is firmly framed as a fiction. The motto chosen for the poem, 'The stretched metre of an antique song', is taken from Shakespeare's Sonnet XVII which ironically foresees a time when the real feeling expressed in his poem will be mocked as a mere poetic fantasy. Placed at the head of the poem, the quotation questions whether *Endymion*'s 'stretching' of the classical tale to over 4,000 lines is nothing more than a 'poet's rage'. The poem's fictiveness is further emphasised by the picture which Keats gives of himself, in the country and far from 'the city's din', beginning to write the poem we are reading, and proposing the timetable for its composition (I. 34–62). Poetry for Keats is in the end fictive, and its assertions perhaps overweeningly arrogant.

An extreme faith in the power of poetry and the imagination is set against an awareness that when measured against our knowledge in time, poetry is *a* truth, but possibly a severely limited one or even one which is finally untrue. That ambiguity is evident throughout Keats's work. It appears in the provisional note of the aspiring early poetry and in the confusions of *Endymion*, though its clearest expression is to be found in the mature work – the odes, *Lamia* and *The Fall of Hyperion* – where it has become an explicit rather than a potential concern.

What ties these speculations, and Keats's poetry, to common experience, is the insistence on truth to 'sensation'. The desire 'for a Life of Sensations rather than of Thoughts' most obviously relates to a recurrent wish to lose the self in being. 'Sensation', however, is more than self-indulgence. It is central to a belief in the veracity of concrete experience. At one extreme it is quite literally the information of our senses. As Keats was to write in April 1819, 'suppose a rose to have sensation, it blooms on a beautiful morning it enjoys itself – but there comes a cold wind, a hot sun – it can not escape it, it cannot destroy its annoyances' (*Letters*, ii. 101). This gives the basis for the characteristic tactile, visual and auditory effects in the poetry, and the preference for metaphors of fullness, of a selfhood bursting with its own identity. Sensation then is linked with Keatsian empathy. Being taken up into sensation, into something deeply other to the self, takes Keats a long way from simple sense experience. For him, sensations are

internal as well as external. 'My sensations are sometimes deadened for weeks together', or again, writing to Reynolds, 'I was to
give you a history of [my] sensations, and day-night mares'
(*Letters*, ii. 146). Keats imagined in sensory terms: the imaginative
experience therefore started from direct experience, but its meaning went beyond mere day-dreaming. It was in fact a kind of
thinking through images. The crux was that the truth once
apprehended was seen to be true. Like Adam's dream it is self-
authenticating. Thus the 'Ode to a Nightingale' both tells one
truth (that poetry reaches back and overcomes time), and poses
against it a counter-truth (that this is only a fiction): it fleetingly
attains a stance which can accommodate contradictory orders of
experience. But the poem must start in the experience of actually
hearing a bird, and end in a truthfulness to the poet's literal
experience – the sense of loss as the bird flies off. It is at once a
day-dream and a 'day-night mare'.

Negative capability, with dependence on sensation and empathic
projection, defines a Romantic polarity opposed to the practice of
Wordsworth and Coleridge. All Romantic artists shared the problem of relating the subjective and the objective. As John Bayley
says, 'the premises on which any romantic poem is written are an
acute consciousness of the isolated creating self on the one hand,
and of a world unrelated, and possibly indifferent and hostile, on the
other; and the wish somehow to achieve a harmonious synthesis of the
two'.[31] Coleridge's response to this problem was analytic and
metaphysical, marked by a fascination with his own mental and
creative processes. Keats, who believed that the poet's ego should go
out into the thing perceived, thought Coleridge, like Wordsworth,
guilty of forcing himself upon both the material and the reader, and
of allowing the self to obtrude upon the impersonality of great poetry.
As Keats was to insist, there is profound difference between his own
genius and that of Wordsworth:

As to the poetical Character itself, (I mean that sort of which, if I am any
thing, I am a Member; that sort distinguished from the wordsworthian
or egotistical sublime; which is a thing per se and stands alone) it is not
itself – it has no self – it is every thing and nothing – It has no
character – it enjoys light and shade; it lives in gusto, be it foul or
fair, high or low, rich or poor, mean or elevated – It has as much delight
in conceiving an Iago as an Imogen. What shocks the virtuous
philosop[h]er, delights the cameleon Poet.   (*Letters*, i. 386–7)

The difficulty of reconciling the amoral creativity of the 'cameleon
Poet' with the demands of truth was in some part answered by the

notion of 'intensity' which Keats puts forward in a letter to his brothers written on 20 December 1817:

the excellence of every Art is its intensity, capable of making all disagreeables evaporate, from their being in close relationship with Beauty & Truth–Examine King Lear & you will find this examplified throughout; but in [Benjamin West's painting, 'Death on the Pale Horse',] we have unpleasantness without any momentous depth of speculation excited, in which to bury its repulsiveness. (*Letters*, i. 192)

Preparing *Endymion* for the press in January 1818, Keats knew that his speculations would take him far beyond the bounds of his pastoral romance – 'I think a little change has taken place in my intellect lately' (*Letters*, i. 214). Although that 'little change' had mapped out an alternative to Coleridgean introspection and Wordsworth's 'egotistical sublime', it offered Keats little immediate help.

The disjointed verse letter which he wrote to J. H. Reynolds in March 1818 reveals a crisis in Keats's thinking. Beginning in a jocose manner, it plays off the grotesque and incoherent wanderings of the fancy in nightmares and daydreams against the beauty to be enjoyed in poetry and painting, before abruptly turning to a vision of nature's alien destructiveness:

> . . . I saw
> Too far into the sea, where every maw
> The greater on the less feeds evermore. –
> But I saw too distinct into the core
> Of an eternal fierce destruction . . .
> Still do I that fierce destruction see –
> The shark at savage prey, the hawk at pounce,
> The gentle robin, like a pard or ounce,
> Ravening a worm. (lines 93–105)

The self-consuming violence of the natural world shocks the imagination which has perceived it by seeing 'Too far into the sea': consciousness of that violence destroys normal human satisfactions:

> . . . is it that imagination brought
> Beyond its proper bound, yet still confined,
> Lost in a sort of purgatory blind,
> Cannot refer to any standard law
> Of either earth or heaven? It is a flaw
> In happiness to see beyond our bourne –

> It forces us in summer skies to mourn;
> It spoils the singing of the nightingale.   (lines 78–85)

Imagination sees beyond the mortal but cannot attain the full perspective of 'heaven's Law'. Its 'purgatory blind' is created by the imagination's ability to conceive the essential violence of natural destruction without being able to understand it. The intensity of art and the imagination cannot make disagreeables evaporate: instead, the awareness it brings may prove disabling and destructive.

Keats's impasse here signals the intellectual and aesthetic crisis he underwent between the autumn and winter of 1818. 'Beauty' was an insufficient answer to suffering and pain. The danger was that the etherealising imagination took too little cognisance of ordinary life. John Wilson, writing in 1819, argued that the decline of poetic drama after the seventeenth century came about because the imagination no longer 'submitted to life'.

The whole character of our life and literature seems to us to show in our cultivated classes a disposition of imagination to separate itself from real life, and to go over into works of art.

The lyric nature of 'the great overflow of poetry in this age may be in part from this cause'.[32] Keats could perceive this limitation clearly enough in the work of Hunt: his difficulty was to find a way beyond it.

4

Hyperion: 'Colossal Grandeur'

Although Keats told Haydon of his intention to write on the story of Hyperion while still working on *Endymion* in January 1818,[1] it was not until the following autumn, after a summer spent touring Scotland with Charles Brown, that he began the poem.[2] Nursing his brother, Tom, who was to die of tuberculosis on 1 December, Keats found that 'His identity presses upon me so . . . I am obliged to write, and plunge into abstract images.' (*Letters*, i. 369). The 'abstract images', like those of *Endymion*, were drawn from classical mythology. Unlike Keats's 'Poetic Romance', *Hyperion* retells the story of an epic struggle, the overthrow of Saturn and the Titans by their children, the Olympian gods. Keats's version begins in mid-action, after the Titans' first defeat. Its central action was to have been the displacement of the Titan sun-god, Hyperion, as yet undefeated, by his successor Apollo. Hyperion's downfall is seen as a tragic consequence of an inevitable historical progress towards higher forms of being. The largest, and most powerful, part of the fragment is devoted to the Titans' suffering (Books I–II): the incomplete Book III describes Apollo's initiation as a god.

In *Hyperion* Keats strove for impersonality and objectivity, trying to avoid the 'deep and sentimental cast' of *Endymion* in favour of 'a more naked and grecian Manner'.[3] 'Naked' indicates that *Hyperion*'s Greek 'Manner' ('artistic style') looks to the example of Hellenic art rather than that of Greek literature. To a remarkable extent Keats was successful. The fragment, written more deliberately than any previous poem, has a chastened and disciplined style which found an important source of inspiration in classical sculpture and in painting as well as in the challenge of Milton's *Paradise Lost*.[4] In its most impressive passages *Hyperion* achieves a remarkable maturity. Its handling of scale and space, its sad sonorities, and its epic tone derive from Keats's study of Milton, but are essentially Keatsian in impact. The 'natural sculpture' of Book I's opening, in which Saturn and Thea are seen at once as gods and as humans, provides a good example.

Deep in the shady sadness of a vale
Far sunken from the healthy breath of morn,
Far from the fiery noon, and eve's one star,
Sat grey-haired Saturn, quiet as a stone,
Still as the silence round about his lair;
Forest on forest hung above his head
Like cloud on cloud. No stir of air was there,
Not so much life as on a summer's day
Robs not one light seed from the feathered grass,
But where the dead leaf fell, there did it rest.
A stream went voiceless by, still deadened more
By reason of his fallen divinity
Spreading a shade: the Naiad 'mid her reeds
Press'd her cold finger closer to her lips.

Along the margin-sand large foot-marks went,
No further than to where his feet had strayed,
And slept there since. Upon the sodden ground
His old right hand lay nerveless, listless, dead,
Unsceptred; and his realmless eyes were closed;
While his bowed head seemed listening to the Earth,
His ancient mother, for some comfort yet.   (I. 1–21)

The first eight lines effortlessly create a vast still setting, and
the second paragraph, with its weighty accretion of negatives
brilliantly held over the line ending ('nerveless, listless, dead, /
Unsceptred'), enacts the oppressive inner desolation of Saturn.
Even here Keats's success is not total. The coy Naiad is an intruder
from *Endymion*'s pastoral world, and, a little later, the famous simile
of forest oaks as 'green-rob'd senators of mighty woods' (I. 73) is
memorable but detachable from its context (as Keats admitted
when he simply excised it from *The Fall of Hyperion*). Structure and
overall effect are subordinated to local 'beauties', Keats's old
danger. Occasional failures in Books I and II are not surprising.
What is remarkable is that while inviting comparison with Milton,
Keats can so often achieve his own effects:

Next Cottus; prone he lay, chin uppermost
As though in pain, for still upon the flint
He ground severe his skull, with open mouth
And eyes at horrid working.   (II. 49–52)

Keats's insistence upon loss and suffering (which may here draw
on memories from his medical experiences) coupled with sympathy for the Titans, humanises the immortal but fallen gods.
This was one of the qualities Keats admired in *Paradise Lost* –

Milton is godlike in the sublime pathetic. In Demons, fallen Angels, and Monsters the delicacies of passion, living in and from their immortality, is of the most softening and dissolving nature.[5]

The connection between Milton and *Hyperion* goes beyond matters of style and technique, as Shelley perceived. He thought that 'the scenery and drawing of [Keats's] Saturn Dethroned, and the fallen Titans, surpassed those of Satan and his rebellious angels in the *Paradise Lost* – possessing more human interest . . . the whole poem [is] supported throughout with a colossal grandeur equal to the subject.'[6] While this is a striking tribute, given Shelley's intimate knowledge of and fervent admiration for Greek literature, his claim that *Hyperion*'s subject is superior to Milton's, because more human, has a suggestive relationship to Keats's own attitudes to Milton. For him, as for the Hunt circle, Milton was exemplary not only as a poet but as a patriot and political hero. When annotating his own copy of *Paradise Lost*, Keats wrote against the description of the eclipse of the sun which 'with fear of change / Perplexes monarchs' (I. 598–9),

How noble and collected an indignation against Kings, '*and for fear of change perplexes Monarchs*', etc. His very wishing should have had power to pull that feeble animal Charles from his bloody throne. 'The evil days' had come to him [i.e. Milton's sufferings after the Restoration]; he hit the new System of things a mighty mental blow; the exertion must have had or is yet to have some sequences.[7]

Precisely how Keats interpreted *Paradise Lost* is not known, but he evidently believed that the epic contained at least local expressions of Milton's republicanism through the figure of Satan, and faced with God's first appearance speaking to the angels in *Paradise Lost* Book III, 135–7, Keats commented tersely, 'Hell is finer than this'.[8] Whether or not Keats believed, like Blake, that Milton was 'of the Devil's party without knowing it', the fact is that the 'vale' in which the Titans suffer and the whole framework of Books I and II of *Hyperion* are a reworking of Milton's portrait of Satan and the fallen angels, except that the Titans are given unambiguous sympathy. Milton's epic is divested of its Christianity, and recast as a pagan poem. *Hyperion* has no concept of Sin, no Christian cosmogony, and no Hell or Satan. It depicts an evolutionary struggle between lower and higher kinds of good, and is at root optimistic, with a progressive view of mankind's history. Keats's 'Greek' myth is not simply an effort to imagine past modes of belief, though it is in part that. On 31 December

1818 he wrote, 'Now to me manners and customs long since passed whether among the Babylonians or the Bactrians are as real, or even more real than those among which I now live – My thoughts have turned lately this way' (*Letters*, ii. 18). Byron, not otherwise an admirer of Keats's poetry, thought *Hyperion* 'seems actually inspired by the Titans, and is as sublime as Aeschylus.'[9] As in *Endymion*, the reanimation of Greek myth is neither antiquarian nor decorative in intention, but a means of exploring beliefs and propositions counter to, or subversive of, conventional religious and political beliefs.

Although Keats was not an atheist or a revolutionary, his first version of the *Hyperion* story implicitly supports a liberal view of both politics and religion. Comparing the projected *Hyperion* with *Endymion*, Keats told Haydon that in the new poem 'the march of passion and endeavour will be undeviating – and one great contrast between them will be – that the Hero of the written tale [i.e., *Endymion*] being mortal is led on, like Buonaparte, by circumstance; whereas the Apollo in Hyperion being a fore-seeing God will shape his actions like one' (*Letters*, i. 207).

Although the fragment Keats wrote reaches no further than Apollo's apotheosis into godhood, 'the march of endeavour and passion' was to have been *Hyperion*'s theme. In the spring preceding the fragment's composition, Keats was particularly exercised by the examples of Wordsworth and Milton. Wordsworth was, he believed, 'deeper than Milton' because 'he did not think into the human heart, as Wordsworth has done' (*Letters*, i. 281, 282). Yet since Milton, as a philosopher,

had sure as great powers as Wordsworth – What is then to be inferr'd? O many things – It proves there is really a grand march of intellect – , It proves that a mighty providence subdues the mightiest Minds to the service of the time being, whether it be in human Knowledge or Religion.
(*Letters*, i. 282)

Paradise Lost, Keats believed, was limited by Milton's inability to transcend seventeenth-century Protestant 'Dogmas and superstitions'. Wordsworth's superiority 'has depended more upon the general and gregarious advance of intellect, than individual greatness of Mind' (*Letters*, i. 281). A year and a half later Keats repeated his optimistic belief in the inevitability of progress. 'All civil[iz]ed countries become gradually more enlighten'd and there should be a continual change for the better', though that change for the better might include temporary reverses. The medieval period saw 'the gradual annihilation of the tyranny of the nobles', but by the seventeenth century the struggle by European Kings 'to destroy all popular privileges' was successful except in England. The English Revolution and Williamite settlement secured against tyranny until, ironically, 'the liberal writers of france and england sowed the seeds of opposition' abroad which 'burst out in the french revolution'. In its turn the French Revolution caused a powerful backlash in Britain: it

gave our Court hopes of turning back to the despotism of the 16 century. They have made a handle of [the French Revolution] in every way to undermine our freedom. They spread a horrid superstition against all inovation and improvement – The present struggle in England of the people is to destroy this superstition.

The French Revolution, then, has put a 'temporary stop to . . . the change for the better'. In September 1819 there were, Keats believed, clear signs that liberal and radical views were going to change the political impasse.[10]

While it is true that Keats himself claimed 'I know very little of these things' (*Letters*, ii. 194) and his expressions of political concern are scattered, they reflect what he and his circle were thinking and are self-consistent. Milton was not only a poetic challenge, one which in the end Keats felt was 'death to me', but was a problematic exemplar. Keats's patriotic conviction of England's heroic role meant that the revolutionary achievements of Cromwell stood as a stark challenge to the stifling oppression and small-mindedness of his own times:

We have no Milton, no Algernon Sidney [a republican admired by liberals who was executed by Charles II] – Governers in these days loose the title of Man in exchange for that of Diplomat and Minister – We breathe in a sort of Officinal Atmosphere – All the departments of Government have strayed far from Simplicity[11] which is the greatest of Strength. (*Letters*, i. 396)

Contemporary politics and politicians lacked sublimity or heroism: Milton had participated in an heroic phase of British history and democracy, and even in defeat had written a poem which 'must have had *or is yet to have* [my italics] some sequences [i.e., effects]'.

Hyperion is not an overtly political poem, but its mythic world puts forward an alternative vision of heroic struggle and eventual human progress, largely formed out of Keats's dissatisfaction with contemporary politics, religion, and government. This was not evident to unsympathetic readers. The *Eclectic Review*'s critic objected to *Hyperion* on the grounds that 'Mr. Keats, seemingly, can think or write of scarcely anything else than the "happy pieties" of Paganism': significantly he concludes his assessment by complaining that the 1820 volume lacks any proof of Christianity or any 'indication that the Author is allied by any one tie to his family, his country, or his kind.'[12] Such a misreading stems from the critic's inability to concede even the possibility that Keats's commitment to Greek myth might be a deliberate effort to escape from the confines of conventional Christianity.

If *Hyperion* is from one point of view an attempt to rewrite *Paradise Lost* in non-Christian terms, Keats also believed that the objectivity of Milton's style and narrative offered a way out of the impasse which he believed modern poetry had reached in Wordsworth. Compared with Milton, Keats questioned 'whether Wordsworth has in truth epic passions, and martyrs himself to the human heart, the main region of his song' (*Letters*, i. 278–9). Was Wordsworth's greater knowledge of the human heart in some way disabling? In the letter written in May 1818, Keats goes on to make his famous comparison of life with 'a large Mansion of Many Apartments'. The second, the 'Chamber of Maiden-Thought', is an *Endymion*-like elysium of intoxicated delight, which, however, eventually sharpens 'one's vision into the heart and nature of Man' and

convinces ones nerves that the World is full of Misery and Heartbreak, Pain, Sickness and oppression – whereby This Chamber of Maiden Thought becomes gradually darken'd and at the same time on all sides of it many doors are set open – but all dark – all leading to dark passages – We see not the ballance of good and evil. We are in a Mist . . . We feel the 'burden of the Mystery'.

Wordsworth's poetry, which is 'deeper than Milton' had progressed this far. 'To this point was Wordsworth come . . . when he wrote "Tintern Abbey" and . . . his genius is explorative of those dark Passages' (*Letters*, i. 281). Yet that knowledge may mean the denial of 'epic passions' and leave the poet a 'martyr' to the 'human heart'. The modern poet's task was to create a poetry which, starting from Wordsworth's deeper knowledge of the human heart, could achieve the epic and heroic grandeur of Milton.

Hyperion's epic structure gives Keats the opportunity to externalise his characters through dialogue, which forms a high proportion of the whole poem, and the example of Milton would, Keats hoped, enable him to create an objectivity which reached beyond the dangerously solipsistic self-consciousness of the modern poet. Yet the poem's underlying theme is the role and function of poetry. The escape from modern self-consciousness was illusory.

Hyperion, though formally a fragment, is in fact coherent and self-contained. Keats's choice of a mythological episode only incompletely recorded by classical writers meant that he was free to invent characters and theme while still having the advantage of working with a story known to his readers. *Hyperion*'s version of the struggle between the Titans and their successors differs from conventional depictions and interpretations. Saturn was usually represented according to Godwin's *Pantheon* as 'a very old man, with a long beard, and bearing a scythe in his hand'. Godwin explains that because of the closeness of the Greek words for Saturn and Time, the two were connected, which explains why Saturn is presented as 'the devourer of his children'.[13] Keats's Saturn is a less ambiguous and fearsome figure. His connection with time is severed, and he is presented as still vigorous and powerful. Keats also runs together the Giants and the Titans – Godwin says, 'As under the reign of Saturn there was a rebellion of the Titans, so under the reign of Jupiter happened the war of the Giants.'[14] By eliding these events, and making Saturn sympathetic, *Hyperion*'s narrative describes the displacement of the pre-Hellenic Titans by their offspring who, led by Jupiter, established the rule of the Olympian gods.

The poem opens with Saturn and his fellow Titans already defeated, and cast down from heaven to a rock-strewn cavernous 'vale' on earth. Hyperion, the sun-god, is the sole exception, and he succeeds in rousing the Titans' almost broken spirits (Books I–II). Book III introduces the figure of Apollo, whom Keats, again imaginatively varying and developing his sources, presents as a human about to be transformed into the Olympian god of the sun, music, and poetry by the Titan goddess of memory, Mnemosyne (who has changed her allegiance, recognising the Olympians' superiority). The obscure events of the wars of the gods have been turned into narrative depicting an inevitable development towards greater perfection. Oceanus' long speech to the fallen Titans in Book II, urging acceptance of their fate, makes this explicit.

> We fall by course of Nature's law, not force
> Of thunder, or of Jove.   (II. 181–2)

Saturn, blinded by his long supremacy as leader of the Titans, has failed to realise that just as he and the Titans were not 'the first of powers', since Chaos and Darkness first gave birth to Light, which in turn created Heaven and Earth, the parents of the Titans themselves, so the Titans cannot be the last (lines 182–201):

> . . . on our heels a fresh perfection treads,
> A power more strong in beauty, born of us
> And fated to excel us . . .   (II. 212–14)

The Olympians 'tower' above their parents, the Titans, in beauty, and

> . . . 'tis the eternal law
> That first in beauty should be first in might.
> Yea, by that law, another race may drive
> Our conquerors to mourn as we do now.   (II. 228–31)

The optimistic belief in an evolutionary progress governed by the ultimate primacy and might of beauty provides a link between the kind of thinking in *Endymion* and Keats's epic. It also suggests how far *Hyperion*'s re-telling of the classical creation myth both reflects on contemporary politics and gives a radical (and non-Christian) re-reading of human history and its possible future.

The poem makes a serious effort to locate its story in historical time. The violent events in 'infant world' of the 'primeval Gods' (I. 26, 292) were seen in the heavens by 'sages and keen-eyed astrologers / Then living on the earth' and their observations recorded on 'remnants huge / Of stone, or marble swart,' even though modern man can no longer read them (I. 277–83). Further, from 'sacred hills' the incense of pagan worshippers rises to Hyperion's palace (I. 186–9). The wars between the Titans and Olympians thus precede the founding of Greek civilisation, and belong to the time of the Chaldeans. The descriptions of Hyperion's palace draw on visual images from ancient Egyptian statuary, as does the figure of Hyperion himself,[15] while his hair 'of short Numidian curl' contrasts with Apollo's 'golden tresses' (III. 131), linking the Titan with Africa. In an even earlier period Coelus (Heaven) and Terra (Earth) held power before being replaced by their offspring the Titans, but though now without power, they still exist as natural forces, able to comfort but not help their fallen children (again, Keats chooses to ignore the tradition of hostility between Coelus and his sons).

In *Hyperion* Keats distinguishes not between good and bad, but between lower and higher kinds of good. In the terms used by Keats in November and December 1817, Saturn is the type of the 'Men of Power' (*Letters*, i. 184) – that is, he has a firm sense of self, and powerful egotistical drives. Hence he speaks desperately of the loss of his 'strong identity' (I. 114) and of his 'real self'. He is regarded elegiacally as a noble but now outmoded force, whose benignant and innocent Saturnian age is now over. Saturn's dependence upon his sense of 'identity' probably links him with Keats's idea of the 'wordsworthian or egotistical sublime' (i. 387), the self-conscious kind of sublimity which *Hyperion* is meant to displace. The parallel is not exact nor is it meant to be. Equally suggestive, though equally imprecise, is the possible connection between Napoleon and Saturn. Keats disagreed with 'the part which the Liberals [e.g., Hazlitt] take in the Cause of Napoleon'. Keats believed that Napoleon had betrayed revolutionary hopes and, worse, taught the modern world 'how to organise their monstrous armies' (*Letters*, i. 397). The parallel Keats drew between Endymion and Napoleon as compared to Apollo – Endymion 'being mortal is led on, like Buonaparte, by circumstance; whereas the Apollo in Hyperion being a fore-seeing God will shape his actions like one' (*Letters*, i. 207) – is instructive. Saturn is not, of course, a man but he is a lesser being than Apollo. Napoleon, certainly one of the 'Men of Power', is not to be directly equated with Saturn, but both are to be superseded.

Apollo is a visionary of another kind. He is the 'Man of Achievement in Literature', a representative of the imaginative powers of negative capability. This kind of poet, the kind with whom Keats identified his own genius, lacks a sense of identity. Sympathetic identification with suffering, joy, even evil, unaccompanied by moral prejudgement, is the essential quality of his 'poetical character':

. . . A Poet is the most unpoetical of any thing in existence; because he has no Identity – he is continually in for – and filling some other Body – The Sun, the Moon, the Sea and Men and Women. (*Letters*, i. 387)

Keats wrote these words in November 1818 as he began to write *Hyperion* (almost immediately the letter refers to Saturn and Ops).

Apollo's transformation into a god is overseen by Mnemosyne, 'an ancient Power' who has

. . . forsaken old and sacred thrones

64

> For prophecies of thee, and for the sake
> Of loveliness new born.   (III. 77–9)

Although Apollo has been given the lyre as an instrument, one whose 'new tuneful wonder' surpasses all earlier instruments (III. 62–7), he still needs the knowledge of suffering and pain before he can assume godhead. That knowledge is supplied by his reading of Mnemosyne's face:

> Mute thou remainest – mute! yet I can read
> A wondrous lesson in thy silent face:
> Knowledge enormous makes a God of me.
> Names, deeds, grey legends, dire events, rebellions,
> Majesties, sovran voices, agonies,
> Creations and destroyings, all at once
> Pour into the wide hollows of my brain,
> And deify me, as if some blithe wine
> Or bright elixir peerless I had drunk,
> And so become immortal.   (III. 111–20)

With 'fierce convulse', Apollo the man dies into his new life as a foreseeing god, the type of the poet of negative capability. While Keats regarded Apollo above all as the god of poetry, morning, and the sun, he was also traditionally the god of healing. The poet-god's function then was to heal and answer suffering and evil as well as to understand.

And then the poem stops. Woodhouse's account of how the epic was to have continued, inadvertently explains why.

> The poem, if completed, would have treated of the dethronement of Hyperion, the former God of the Sun, by Apollo – and incidentally, of those of Oceanus by Neptune, of Saturn by Jupiter, etc. – and of the war of the Giants [i.e., Titans] for Saturn's re-establishment, with other events, of which we have but very dark hints in the mythological poets of Greece and Rome. In fact, the incidents would have been pure creations of the poet's brain.[16]

The action of the poem reaches its climax with Apollo's apotheosis. Anything more would have been redundant. The struggle between Apollo and the Titans is really an inner one. *Hyperion*'s drama could not survive Apollo's attainment of godhead since there was no way of disguising the correspondence between Keats's own aspirations and Apollo's symbolic role. The point once made could only be repeated. There was no room to invent more.

Apart from that there was another problem. A major shortcoming in Book III is Keats's inability to create a credible diction for Apollo ('blithe wine' and 'bright elixir peerless' belong to *Endymion*). This is coupled with a failure to specify the nature of Apollo's new-found knowledge – the marvellously Keatsian line, all feel, 'Pour into the wide hollows of my brain', is supported only by a resonant catalogue of generalities. The only 'Muse' Keats can invoke is the one which *Hyperion* set out to reject.

> . . . O Muse! . . .
> Meantime touch piously the Delphic harp,
> And not a wind of heaven but will breathe
> In aid soft warble from the Dorian flute;
> For lo! 'tis for the Father of all verse.
> Flush every thing that hath a vermeil hue,
> Let the rose glow intense and warm the air,
> And let the clouds of even and of morn
> Float in voluptuous fleeces o'er the hills;
> Let the red wine within the goblet boil,
> Cold as a bubbling well; let faint-lipped shells,
> On sands, or in great deeps, vermilion turn
> Through all their labyrinths; and let the maid
> Blush keenly, as with some warm kiss surprised.
>
> (III. 7–22)

This suffers from both the obscurity and the self-excitement of *Endymion*. The idea is that the world should flush with pleasure at the rise of the sun-god Apollo, 'the Father of all verse'. The poeticisms ('soft warble', 'vermeil hue') and the luxuriating adjectives ('voluptuous fleeces', 'faint-lipped shells', 'warm kiss'), like the violent oxymoron of red wine boiling yet remaining cold, mark Keats's reversion to a poetry of 'sensation'. As the blushing 'maid' indicates, this is the world of Endymion. The limits of Keats's own knowledge have been reached: Apollo's apotheosis can be no more than a promissory gesture. Keats has no style, other than a reversion to Endymionese, to deal with Apollo's experience.

Such an account leaves Hyperion, who gives the poem its title, in limbo. Yet he is Keats's other self in the narrative. Hyperion, after Jupiter's victory, is, with the other Titans, cast peremptorily into despair – 'I cannot see – but darkness, death and darkness' (I. 242). Hyperion, like Keats faced with the illness of his brother or his realisation that to look too directly at the 'fierce destruction' of nature might incapacitate the imagination, has no adequate response. The Wordsworthian impasse turns out to be Keats's as well.

Yet this first version of the Hyperion story does contain within itself a suggestion of a possible way forward. It is clear enough that the Titans' sufferings are the centre of the epic fragment's human and psychological interest, and are realised with an intense simplicity unavailable for the presentation of Apollo. Keats's empathic depiction of the Titans leads him to perceive a dialectical relationship between suffering and consciousness, between 'the knowledge of evil and the knowledge of self'.[17] Oceanus, recognising the inevitability of the Titans' defeat, advises them that

> . . . to bear all naked truths,
> And to envisage circumstance, all calm,
> That is the top of sovereignty.   (II. 203–5)

This is not simply an advocacy of stoicism. Rather, Oceanus sees that there is a connection between pain or sorrow and its apparent opposite, beauty. That is evident elsewhere in the poem. In Thea's face sorrow makes 'Sorrow more beautiful than Beauty's self' (I. 36). Clymene, describing to the assembled Titans the power of Apollo's 'new blissful golden melody' which is full 'of calm joy', says her own efforts to create 'songs of misery' on a 'mouthed shell' which might express their misery, were overwhelmed by Apollo's lyre. 'A living death was in each gush of sounds' which made her 'sick / Of joy and grief at once' (II. 262–95). Her mingling of joy and grief, which recognises the superiority of Apollo's mandate while lamenting the passing of Saturn's supremacy, is a self-denying acceptance of change and suffering, is indeed the knowledge to which Apollo aspires. Joy and suffering, beauty and transience, are, she realises, indivisible.

The fissure between belief in an evolutionary Darwinian aestheticism in a world of 'abstract images' and the reality of his brother Tom's painfully prolonged dying, could not be contained within Keats's 'objective' epic. While he later returned to this material, and with greater success, *Hyperion*'s style and subject matter reach a new level. It was a direction Keats could not follow any further (*The Fall of Hyperion*, though it uses parts of the earlier material, is a quite different poem).

5

Four 'medieval' love stories

Isabella, *The Eve of St Agnes*, and 'La Belle Dame sans Merci', and the sonnet on Paolo and Francesca are very different poems and written at different times. *Isabella* was begun in March 1818, immediately after the completion of *Endymion*, and finished by 27 April. *The Eve of St Agnes*, whose subject was proposed by Mrs Isabella Jones, was composed between 18 January and 2 February 1819 in the period following Keats's concentrated work on *Hyperion*. The two short poems were written in mid April 1819, shortly before the major odes. However, all tell love stories, all are 'modern' recreations of a medieval source or setting, and none of them offers a self-evident 'meaning'. They are also alike in that the versions of the poems available to nineteenth and twentieth-century readers are not necessarily those which Keats would have chosen to perpetuate. On two occasions he said that he did not want to publish *Isabella* at all.[1] Both 'La Belle Dame' and the sonnet were excluded from the 1820 volume, but published in Hunt's *Indicator* with substantive variations from the now accepted text. The final form of *Isabella* was only reached with help and advice from his friend Reynolds, from his publisher, John Taylor, and from Richard Woodhouse, while Tayor and Woodhouse were instrumental in ensuring that Keats's earlier, less explicit, version of *The Eve of St Agnes* was chosen for the public of 1820 and today.

The evidence of the drafts and the poems' publishing history demonstrate that Keats's anxieties about *Isabella*, *The Eve of St Agnes*, and 'La Belle Dame' turned on his fear of serious readers, and reviewers in particular, finding them sentimental. Less consciously, his uncertainties were bound up with the rifts and confusions in his own attitude to women and sexuality. The four stories are about couples possessed by love, though differently possessed and possessing. They all have strong erotic elements, and in two of them, *Isabella* and 'La Belle Dame', the intensity of sexual love leads to death. In all four fulfilment cannot take place within the human or natural world, hence their movements towards unconsciousness, dreaming, or death. The women are of two types, either passively responding to events outside their control, or, in the case of La Belle Dame, dominant and demonic. Viewed reductively, they are expressions of prevalent attitudes to women's sexuality. La Belle Dame's overwhelming sexuality destroys men; Isabella's violent love can only be fulfilled through her death; the passive and innocent Madeline is taken by her male lover, Porphyro; Paolo and Francesca are condemned to suffer in hell for their carnal love. A bare account of their themes does scant justice to the ambiguously balanced poems Keats actually wrote, but does show how closely they resemble the uncritical transformation of conventional, sexual fantasy into safely ingenuous 'poetic' romances.

Keats was the more aware of this risk because of the confusions in his own attitude to women. It is quite clear that Keats the man strongly polarised male and female qualities. Equally, perhaps consequentially, he both idealised women and regarded them as inferior to men. Yet he knew his feelings were muddled. He wrote to Benjamin Bailey on 18 July 1818,

> . . . I am certain I have not a right feeling towards Women – at this moment I am striving to be just to them but I cannot – Is it because they fall so far beneath my Boyish imagination? When I was a Schoolboy I though[t] a fair Woman a pure Goddess, my mind was a soft nest in which some one of them slept thought she knew it not – I have no right to expect more than their reality. I thought them etherial above Men – I find them [written 'then'] perhaps equal.
>
> (*Letters*, i. 341)

This youthful idealisation is expressed, directly and callowly, in the early Spenserian romances:

> . . . young Calidore is burning
> To hear of knightly deeds, and gallant spurning
> Of all unworthiness; and how the strong of arm
> Kept off dismay, and terror, and alarm
> From lovely woman: while brimful of this,
> He gave each damsel's hand so warm a kiss,
> And had such manly ardour in his eye,
> That each at other looked half-staringly;
> And then their features started into smiles
> Sweet as blue heavens o'er enchanted isles.
>
> ('Calidore', lines 142–51)

This transparent mixture of idealisation and self-excitement, disguised as 'romance', would not be worth quoting except that Keats chose to publish 'Calidore' in *Poems* (1817). Similar poems can be found in the magazines of the time. Knight-errantry was a fashionable poetic pose, a playful but clear expression of the dependence of 'fair Women' upon men's protection. Keats's does no more than reflect his society's commonplace attitude: he differs only in the seriousness with which he took such fictions.

By the time he wrote *Isabella*, Keats had rejected this kind of romance. Shortly before beginning the poem he wrote to Bailey,

'Why should Woman suffer?' Aye. Why should she? . . . These things are, and he who feels how incompetent the most skyey Knight errantry is [written 'its'] to heal this bruised fairness is like a sensitive leaf on the hot hand of thought. (*Letters*, i. 209)

'Knight errantry' will not do in the face of reality, but Keats has still not freed himself from a condescending solicitude towards women's weakness ('bruised fairness').

At one extreme Keats was revolted by the grossness of sexual desire. In his copy of Burton's *Anatomy of Melancholy*, given him by Charles Brown in 1819, he wrote:

Here is the old plague spot; the pestilence, the raw scrofula. I mean that there is nothing disgraces me in my own eyes so much as being one of a race of eyes nose and mouth beings in a planet call'd the earth who all from Plato to Wesley have always mingled goatish winnyish lustful love with the abstract adoration of the deity. I don't understand Greek – is the love of God and the love of women express'd in the same word in Greek? I hope my little mind is wrong – if not I could – Has Plato separated these loves? Ha! I see how they endeavour to divide – But there appears to be a horrid relationship.[2]

This is in flat contradiction of *Endymion*'s whole argument for the transforming power of human love. 'Lustful love' and love of the immortal are incompatible. In another marginal note to Burton he said:

The Barbarians stand in awe of a fair woman, and at a beautiful aspect a fierce Spirit is pacified

'abash'd the devil stood'[3]

These extraordinary outbursts are an extreme expression of a morality which idealised women's innocence, purity, and beauty at the cost of denying their sexuality. Keats's innermost drives were defined by the conventional prescriptions. *Endymion*'s vision of a liberated sexuality is threatened by an unconscious fear of releasing the libido's energies. Keats was bound by the very attitudes from which he struggled to free himself. In one sense, his poems on love and women are expressions of the ultimate consequences of those attitudes. If women are either goddesses or enchantresses, and sexuality is to be feared, then the fulfilment of human love is a kind of death. The equation is one repeatedly made in the poetry's imagery, and is openly stated in his letters to Fanny Brawne:

I have two luxuries to brood over in my walks, your Loveliness and the hour of my death. O that I could have possession of them both in the same minute. I hate the world: it batters too much the wings of my self-will, and would I could take a sweet poison from your lips to send me out of it. From no others would I take it. (*Letters*, ii. 133)

While these feelings can be partly excused by the pressures upon Keats – he had no secure career, was desperately in love, and may already have been suffering from the early effects of his fatal illness – the movement towards death as fulfilment is strong in the poetry. The sonnet, 'Why did I laugh tonight', written shortly after *The Eve of St Agnes*, concludes,

> Verse, Fame, and Beauty are intense indeed,
> But Death intenser – Death is Life's high meed.[4]

The confusion in Keats's feelings for Fanny Brawne, resulting from an irrational jealousy coupled with a fear that love and poetry were mutually exclusive commitments, is evident from the letters and from the intensely private and uncontrolled late lyrics addressed to her.[5]

Keats fought against his contradictory emotions. After remarking upon his lack of a 'right feeling towards Women', he told Bailey,

I must absolutely get over this – but how? The only way is to find the root of evil, and so cure it 'with backward mutters of dissevering Power' [*Comus*, line 817]. That is a difficult thing; for an obstinate Prejudice can seldom be produced but from a gordian complication of feelings, which must take time to unravell and care to keep unravelled.

(*Letters*, i. 342)

The quotation from *Comus* makes clear that Keats felt himself unable to establish a proper relation between 'lust' and 'adoration'. In *Comus* these words are spoken by the Attendant Spirit after the Brothers have allowed the evil enchanter to escape: the 'backward mutters' are a charm to free the Lady, that is, Chastity, from Comus' fetters. Keats then is an unclean Comus, and it is his 'gordian' sexual feelings which prevent him from having a 'proper feeling' towards women. (Strikingly, the word 'gordian' is later used to describe the strange beauty of Lamia (I. 47), Keats's last temptress figure.)

Elsewhere Keats saw *Comus* differently. A few months earlier he had written to Reynolds, 'who could gainsay [Milton's] ideas on virtue, vice, and Chastity in Comus, just at the time of the dismissal of Cod-pieces and a hundred other disgraces?' (*Letters*, i. 281–2). The implication seems clear: Keats, a progressive nineteenth-century liberal, *does* gainsay Milton's repressive views on virtue, vice, and chastity. (Milton, that is, over-reacted, understandably enough, against the dissolute excesses of his time.) *Endymion*, with its belief in the generative power of human love, both physical and ideal, is, at it were, Keats's reply to *Comus*. While preparing his long poem for the press, Keats told Reynolds on 19 February 1818, 'it is a false notion that more is gained by receiving than giving – no the receiver and the giver are equal in their benefits . . . and who shall say between Man and Woman which is the most delighted?' (*Letters*, i. 232). This unaffected acknowledgement of the mutuality of sensual love expresses an essential sanity and balance, a balance which Keats, under pressure from his own inner turmoil and from society's assumptions, found very hard to attain.

The difficulty in writing poetry describing erotic and sensual feelings, as Keats knew, was to find a diction and style which could present these kinds of emotional experience satisfactorily, avoiding either coyness or coarseness:

> . . . I shall persist in not publishing The Pot of Basil – It is too smokeable . . . There is too much inexperience of life [written 'live'] in it – which might do very well after one's death – but not while one is alive. There are very few would look to the reality. I intend to use more finesse with the Public. It is possible to write fine things which cannot be laugh'd at in any way. Isabella is what I should call were I a reviewer 'A weak-sided Poem' with an amusing sober-sadness about it. Not that I do not think Reynolds and you are quite right about it – it is enough for me. But this will not do to be public – If I may say so, in my dramatic capacity I enter fully into the feeling: but in Propria Persona I should be apt to quiz it myself – There is no objection of this kind to Lamia – A good deal to St Agnes Eve – only not so glaring. (*Letters*, ii. 174)

This was written on 22 September 1819 to Richard Woodhouse, acting as a go-between for the poet and his publisher, John Taylor. A few days earlier Keats had told Woodhouse that he now thought Isabella 'Mawkish', a word which the lawyer went to the trouble of explaining:

The feeling of mawkishness seems to me to be that which comes upon us where any thing of great tenderness & excessive simplicity is met with when we are not in a sufficiently tender & simple frame of mind to bear it: when we experience a sort of revulsion, or resiliency (if there be such a word) from the sentiment or expression. Now I believe there is nothing in any of the most passionate parts of Isabella to excite this feeling. It may, as may Lear, leave the reader far behind: but there is none of that sugar & butter sentiment, that cloys & disgusts.   (*Letters*, ii. 162)

Keats's strong reaction against *Isabella*, completed but not revised seventeen months earlier, was entirely due to his fears of its critical reception. In the same conversation he told Woodhouse that he wanted to make the bedroom scene in *The Eve of St Agnes* sexually explicit –

He says he does not want ladies to read his poetry: that he writes for men . . . that he sh^d despise a man who would be such an eunuch in sentiment as to leave a maid [i.e., Madeline], with that Character about her, in such a situation.   (*ibid.*, ii. 163)

It is clear that Keats felt there was an unbridgeable divide between poetry's fashionable drawing-room readership and the audience which took poetry seriously. *Isabella* would, he feared, be taken for a 'feminine' poem of 'tenderness & excessive simplicity'. John Hamilton Reynolds, reviewing *Endymion*, said:

There is not one poet of the present day, that enjoys any popularity that will live; each writes for his booksellers and the ladies of fashion, and not for the voice of centuries.[6]

These sentiments were wholly shared by Keats, which explains the violence of his response (if not its ugly 'manliness'). Woodhouse speaks on behalf of the 'ladies', an audience of critical importance to Taylor as a publisher.

What is striking is that Keats's rejection of *Isabella* is only partial, and based on tactical considerations. 'It is enough for me', he says, Reynolds and Woodhouse are 'quite right about it', and the poem 'might do very well after one's death – but not while one is alive.' Keats was convinced that the public of late 1819 would misread the poem's simplicity: 'There are very few who would look to the reality.' In that he was proved wrong and Woodhouse right. Reviewers praised *Isabella* for its depiction of feeling and passion, and for its 'naked and affecting simplicity which goes irresistibly to the heart.'[7]

Keats's divided response to *Isabella* and *The Eve of St Agnes* in September 1819 does, however, reflect a real division in contemporary readers of poetry. The antipathy between Byron's urbanity ('male') and the simplicity and tenderness of feeling sought by Hunt and the early Keats ('female') ran deep, as Keats realised. Of *Don Juan*, which he read later, Keats said, 'the tendency of Byron's poetry is based on a paltry originality, that of being new by making solemn things gay and gay things solemn.'[8] Keats's turning against Hunt and his determination to write with greater knowledge of life, led him, when seeking to change *The Eve of St Agnes* in September 1819, to mistake the true nature of his poetic sensibility, which was close to Hunt's and antipathetic to Byron's worldliness.

Ironically, it was precisely because Keats's own early taste so closely resembled that of 'fashionable' young ladies (his enjoyment of Mrs Tighe's *Psyche*, his early Spenserian poems, and album verses like 'To Some Ladies' are clear proof of that), that the 'romances' written in 1818 and the early part of 1819 are able to expand the 'innocence' of romance into poems which simultaneously affirm and question the truthfulness to experience of persistent patterns in Romantic (and romantic) erotic fantasies. Although these poems bear a strong surface resemblance to conventional romances, they do not use the form for inert wish-fulfilment, but present their stories with an emotional precision which involves the reader at the same time that they provide a definitive, but distanced, realisation of romantic motifs. It is the necessary element of collusion on the reader's part which tells against the current (and fashionable) readings of *The Eve of St Agnes* and 'La Belle Dame sans Merci' as 'anti-romances', which ironically undercut the dreamer's trust in fancy.[9] Unless Keats himself entered the special world of these poems 'innocently' and trustingly, his need to prove his manliness leads him to intrude upon the privacy of the reader's will to believe, a will to believe which is qualified by the stories' own awareness of their fictive limits. The disastrous changes Keats proposed for *The Eve of St Agnes* and the awkward self-divisions in *Lamia* show the dangers of Keats's authorial self-defensiveness all too clearly. The strength of these poems lies in their recognition that, whether they like it or not, Keats and the Western reader are inheritors of a tradition which insists that love and erotic satisfaction should be identical.

The nobility of this idea has a powerful attraction, and reality enough: but it also brings with it the darker possibilities of self-destructiveness, self-denial, or the violences of possessiveness. If Keats's romances exclude the everyday world, it is because the notion of freely chosen love must ignore the very obvious social and material limitations upon that 'choice'. The world, by and large, did not, and does not, endorse romantic simplicity. These four poems testify to the consequent strains, tensions, and burdens it places upon both men and women. What the poems refuse to do is to deny that the dangers and potential destructiveness may be essential if mutual fulfilment is to be a possibility. Keats fears that to expect this kind of exclusive love between man and woman may be yet another instance of mankind asking for the moon. Where *Endymion* believes that we *can* have the moon, the sonnet on Paolo and Francesca can only depict the apparently immutable opposition between reality and the dream of love.

Isabella, first drafted between early March and 27 April 1818, immediately after *Endymion*, may have been suggested by a remark of Hazlitt's in a lecture on Dryden and Pope: 'I should think that a translation of some of the other serious tales in Boccaccio . . . as that of Isabella . . . if executed with taste and spirit, could not fail to succeed in the present day.'[10] Keats originally intended his remaking of the story from the *Decameron* to be part of a joint volume of such tales written with J. H. Reynolds. Italian tales such as Hunt's *The Story of Rimini* (1816) enjoyed a minor vogue and by a coincidence, Barry Cornwall's *Sicilian Story*, based on the same novella as *Isabella*, was published in the same year as Keats's poem. The origins of *Isabella* suggest that Keats, for all his later protests, was aiming for a particular public, the nature of which is clear from a letter to his young sister in which he says, 'I wish the Italian would supersede french in every School throughout the Country for that is full of real Poetry and Romance of a kind more fitted for the Pleasure of Ladies than perhaps our own [or French]' (*Letters*, i. 155).

Yet the story he chose was one of grotesque physical and psychological violence, which his treatment heightens rather than diminishes. The plot is stark and simple. Isabella and Lorenzo, an employee of her two brothers, fall in love. The brothers, who disapprove, murder Lorenzo and bury him secretly. Led by a dream, Isabella finds the corpse, cuts off its head, and hides it at home in a 'garden pot' under a bush of basil. Her brothers discover her secret, deprive her of it, and Isabella dies of grief. Boccaccio's coolly factual narrative gives little in the way of explanation or motive: the brothers find this 'stolen Love' 'highly displeasing', but allow it to continue for a time so that 'no scandal might ensue to them or their Sister, no evil Act being (as yet) committed' (for the medieval audience the fact that the love was secret and Lorenzo servant to the brothers would be sufficient cause for their enmity). However, the translation used by Keats adds a heading which reads, 'Wherein is plainly proved, That Love cannot be rooted up, by any Humane Power or Providence: especially in such a Soul, where it hath been really apprehended.'[11]

In a sense, that is the 'moral' of Keats's romance. But his omissions and additions to Boccaccio's tale create a very different effect. Keats's remark that in 'his dramatic capacity' he entered 'fully into the feeling' singles out the essential change. *Isabella* is not really dramatic, but in its most powerful passages the poem forces the reader to enter into the heroine's feelings. In stanza 51 Isabella and her nurse return with the head –

> In anxious secrecy they took it home,
>   And then the prize was all for Isabel.
> She calmed its wild hair with a golden comb,
>   And all around each eye's sepulchral cell
> Pointed each fringèd lash; the smeared loam
>   With tears, as chilly as a dripping well,
> She drenched away – and still she combed, and kept
> Sighing all day – and still she kissed, and wept.

This bears a close family resemblance to the sensationalism of *grand guignol*: the difference is that the reader experiences not a horrified thrill, but observes and feels with Isabella. It is, after all, Isabella's experience. The dreadful 'prize was all for Isabel': quite, it can be a prize for no one else. The 'prize' is, with terrible irony, all that Isabella can now attain: only she can prize it at its true worth to her. Only she could point with love and tenderness 'each fringed lash' of the 'sepulchral cells' which once contained Lorenzo's eyes.

However, it is not immediately obvious that a sympathetic reading is the proper one if the stanza is taken out of context of the whole poem. A girl taking 'home' the head of her dead lover is bad enough, but when the poet gives the head posthumous life ('She calmed its wild hair'), and slows down the verse with poetically stressed words, repetition, parallelism, assonance, alliteration, inverted word order, and syntax hanging over the line endings –

> Pointed each fringèd lash; the smearèd loam
>   With tears, as chilly as a dripping well,
> She drenched away – | and still she combed, and kept |
> Sighing all day – | and still she kissed, and wept. |

76

– it might seem that everything is being done for sensation. But Keats's choice of *ottava rima*, whose limited choice of rhyme words (ABABABCC), and final couplet creates a self-enclosed stanza, have an odd relation to the inexorable swiftness of the plot itself. Edward Thomas observed that 'each stanza is complete in itself . . . *Isabella* became with the help of the adagio stanza a very still poem.'[12] (One cause of Keats's reaction against *Isabella* was, no doubt, its use of *ottava rima* for a poem of feeling, just at the time *Beppo* and *Don Juan* had claimed the stanza for a serio-jocose idiom.) Stillness and isolation are keys to the poem's effect, as is clear from Keats's alterations to his source. If Boccaccio's narration is sparing of circumstantial detail, Keats's poem is even more so. In the *Decameron* Lorenzo gradually falls in love with Isabella, and, observing her 'by degrees from time to time gave over all the Beauties in the City, which might allure any Affection from him'. In *Isabella* there are no rivals and there is no preamble. The poem opens with two exclamations instead of sentences, defining the heroine and hero in a timeless present which demands the reader's instant sympathy for a simple and tender love:

> Fair Isabel, poor simple Isabel!
> Lorenzo, a young palmer in Love's eye!

Their love is something given, as is its tenderness:

> With every morn their love grew tenderer,
> With every eve deeper and tenderer still.   (lines 9–10)

Where Boccaccio chose to begin with Isabella's brothers (three of them, an unnecessary quota which Keats sensibly reduced to two), *Isabella* sets the bliss of young love against the subsequent pain and distortions of loss.

Keats's division of Boccaccio's tale into a diptych of before and after involves a further radical change. In an extreme situation, Boccaccio's heroine behaves rationally. After Lorenzo's appearance in her dream, she obtains 'favour of her Brethren, to ride a days journey from the City, in company of her trusty Nurse, who . . . knew the secret passages of her Love' (Isabella, however, slips away, her absence 'unsurmised', with her 'aged nurse' who may or may not know of her love), with the intention of secretly bestowing 'honourable Enterment' on her dead lover's corpse. 'Wisdom and government' instruct her that this ambition will be beyond her abilities. At best she can be 'possessed of a part': she therefore takes a 'keen Razor with her', to divide 'the Head from the Body'. Where Boccaccio's heroine dies of 'an extreme Sickness, occasioned only by her ceaseless weeping' and waters the basil plant not only with her tears but also with 'Rose-water, or water distilled from the Flowers of Oranges', Keats makes it entirely clear that *Isabella* goes mad.

On waking from her dream Keats reports, '"Ha! ha!" said she', a forerunner of the 'melodious chuckle in the strings/ Of her lone voice' with which, at the end of the poem, she asks wandering pilgrims about the whereabouts of her lost pot of basil. As they look for the body, her nurse notices Isabella's hectic over-excitement, and is shown a knife which proves too blunt to remove her lover's head with ease:

> How [Isabella] doth whisper to that aged dame,
> And, after looking round the champaign wide,
>   Shows her a knife. – 'What feverous hectic flame
> Burns in thee, child? – What good can thee betide,
>   That thou shouldst smile again?' (lines 346–50)

The bluntness of Isabella's 'knife' heightens the physical grotesquerie of Keats's source. The overall shift from the medieval to the modern version leads to a lingering portrayal of the deed's physical horror.

Where the English translation says that head 'was (as yet) not so much consumed, but by the Locks of Hair, they knew it to be *Lorenzo*'s', Keats writes,

> The thing was vile with green and livid spot,
> And yet they knew it was Lorenzo's face.
>
> (lines 475–6)

Keats's version also cuts out the 'many other Friends' and 'Neighbours' who in Boccaccio observe the heroine's distress: unlike Millais's painting of *Isabella* (1848–9), Keats's poem is as far as possible empty of viewers. The claustrophobic physical and mental violence is all, its effect sharpened by the contrast between the tender idyll of the poem's first part and the suffering of the final movement.

The authorial interpolations which Keats added to the tale stress the gap between Boccaccio's simple medieval factuality and the obstacles facing a modern teller of the story. Stanza 49 is cast in the form of an apparent apology for the need to describe the corpse's decapitation:

> Ah! wherefore all this wormy circumstance?
>> Why linger at the yawning tomb so long?
> O for the gentleness of old Romance,
>> The simple plaining of a minstrel's song!
> Fair reader, at the old tale take a glance,
>> For here, in truth, it doth not well belong
> To speak – O turn thee to the very tale,
> And taste the music of that vision pale.

In part the reference to Boccaccio is an apology (the story is that of an earlier writer), and in part a claim for veracity. But the simplicity and 'gentleness of old Romance' were able to convert these events into the music of a 'vision pale': the modern teller either cannot speak at all or must, as the ensuing stanzas testify, dwell on 'wormy circumstance'. The eloquence of Boccaccio's 'quiet glooms' for 'such a piteous theme' cannot be reproduced by the modern poet (lines 145–52), who can only honour the Italian poet by the attempt to echo him 'in the north wind' (that is, cold and brutal English verse). To attempt to 'make old prose in modern rhyme more sweet' is described as a 'mad assail' (lines 155–6): this, given that Keats's use of antithesis and repetition deliberately flouts Leigh Hunt's proscription of these devices,[13] claims that it is a 'crime' for the modern poet to attempt to 'sweeten' medieval stories as Hunt had done. Hunt falsely 'romanticises' such stories (at the time of writing *Isabella* Keats said, 'It is a great Pity that People should by associating themselves with the fine[st] things, spoil them – Hunt has damned . . . Masks and Sonnets and italian tales' (*Letters*, i. 251–2)). Contemporary poetry must deal with the horror and the 'wormy circumstance'.

The 'wormy circumstance' cannot be blinkered: yet there is a truth about feeling in the story which can only be reached at through the refracted image of literary forms. That essential truth is a psychological truth (what Keats meant when he said he entered 'fully into the feeling'), but one whose necessary manner of expression always risks lapsing into the ridiculous.

> Soon she turned up a soiled glove, whereon
>> Her silk had played in purple phantasies,
> She kissed it with a lip more chill than stone,
>> And put it in her bosom, where it dries
> And freezes utterly unto the bone
>> Those dainties made to still an infant's cries:
> Then 'gan she work again, nor stayed her care,

But to throw back at times her veiling hair.

(lines 369–76)

As often, Keats's images of women's breasts cause difficulties. John Scott commented on those periphrastic 'dainties made to still an infant's cries',

Young ladies, who know, of course, little or nothing of the economy of the nursery, will be apt, we imagine, to pout at this periphrasis, which puts their charms on a level with baby-corals [teething rings]![14]

Scott's own euphemism ('their charms') indicates that he shared Keats's problems, but he was right to see a failure in this line. Keats's rejected attempt to put things right by replacing the phrase with 'Love's sighful throne' would have made things worse: as it stands, it is at least possible to see that Keats wanted to set up an ironic counterpoint between a lover's response and that of the children born from the fulfilment of mutual love. (Unlike Scott, Keats assumes that 'Young ladies' understand the physiological functions of their own bodies.) The local failure is offset by the stanza's overall success. Isabella's 'work', horrific as it seems to the reader, is for her just that: unconscious of how she might be seen, intent on her purpose, she labours to uncover Lorenzo. Her unself-consciousness and total absorption in her task is exactly caught in the final line which faces and defeats the risk of bathos:

> . . . nor stayed her care
> But to throw back at times her veiling hair.

For Isabella, driven into unreason, pursues a need which she cannot question. The last part of the poem (stanzas 48 to the end) portrays someone mentally deranged, permanently so, but whose actions make perfect internal sense. Keats's contrived 'romance' presents the heroine without judgement and, more importantly, without the momentary revulsion or fear most of us experience, however unwillingly, when confronted with the mad. By a very different route, intuitive but apparently self-indulgent and self-luxuriating where Wordsworth is gleeful and severe, *Isabella*, like 'The Idiot Boy', is an empathic portrayal of madness and the extremities of love. The romance has its basis in sensation and the projection of the self into another's feelings.

Isabella is not a perfectly realised poem, but is all the more interesting for that reason. In consequence the poem's central theme is hard to discern. One of the most important changes

Keats made to his source, the introduction of an attack upon capitalist wealth, points to what might have been a possible centre:

14

With her two brothers this fair lady dwelt,
    Enriched from ancestral merchandise,
And for them many a weary hand did swelt
    In torched mines and noisy factories,
And many once proud-quivered loins did melt
    In blood from stinging whip – with hollow eyes
Many all day in dazzling river stood,
To take the rich-ored driftings of the flood.

15

For them the Ceylon diver held his breath,
    And went all naked to the hungry shark;
For them his ears gushed blood; for them in death
    The seal on the cold ice with piteous bark
Lay full of darts; for them alone did seethe
    A thousand men in troubles wide and dark:
Half-ignorant, they turned an easy wheel,
That set sharp racks at work to pinch and peel.

The brothers' 'vision' is 'covetous and sly' (line 141), they are 'jealous' that the lovers are 'blithe and glad' (lines 164–6), are 'Baälites of pelf' (line 451), and wish to marry their sister to 'some high noble and his olive-trees' (line 168). Their 'murderous spite' springs from 'pride and avarice' (lines 293–4). Half-ignorant of the sources of their wealth, 'self-retired / In hungry pride and gainful cowardice', these commercial imperialists are jealous and fearful of the joys and mutuality of love, and its threat to their own advancement. Keats's reworking of Boccaccio's story depicts the brothers' world of commerce and social climbing as actively inimical towards love. The opposition between commercialism and love is, as the reference to 'noisy factories' suggests, one which prevails in the author's own world (a rejected stanza makes the connection obvious by characterising the brothers as free from 'all suspicion of Romantic spleens'[15]). But the story's 'piteous theme' (line 152) allows love no fulfilment but in death. Lorenzo's 'ruddy tide' (line 44) of passion and his being 'flush with love' (line 215) may be contrasted with the 'sick and wan' faces of the brothers (line 213), but it is 'these men of cruel clay' who 'Cut Mercy with a sharp knife to the bone' (line 174).

Although the poem underlines the brothers' moral poverty with heavy irony ('Each richer by his being a murderer', line 224),

Lorenzo's 'great love' ceases in the forest (line 218). Love, suffering, and death belong together. In the opening section of the poem undeclared love causes 'sick longing' (line 23), Isabella's 'untouched cheek' falls ill (lines 33–4), and Lorenzo 'anguishes' through a 'dreary night of love and misery' (line 50). Even when their love is known to one another, Isabella, alone in her chamber, sings a 'ditty fair' of 'delicious love and honeyed dart' (lines 77–8). The description of the lovers' 'Great bliss' and 'great happiness' is followed by an ominous interpolation by the narrator. Its function is to anticipate the outcome (the poem is full of such effects, most famously in the image of the two brothers riding out from Florence with 'their murdered man', line 209): 'the general award of love' is that the 'little sweet doth kill much bitterness' (lines 97–8): the brief joys of love are a sufficient answer to subsequent grief, and were so even in the case of Isabella's 'great distress' and Lorenzo's gruesome exhumation.

What the narrator says is oddly weighted. He begins by asking whether Isabella and Lorenzo could have been unhappy even when their love was unthreatened and at its height. The question, which seems to be that proposed by a modern consciousness, is immediately, and vehemently, denied. Subsequent generations of readers of this and many other 'doleful stories' have invested 'too much of pity' and 'too many tears' for it to be possible for the lovers to have been other than happy (lines 89–96). The next stanza, however, looks in another direction.

> But, for the general award of love,
>   The little sweet doth kill much bitterness;
> Though Dido silent is in under-grove,
>   And Isabella's was a great distress,
> Though young Lorenzo in warm Indian clove
>   Was not embalmed, this truth is not the less –
> Even bees, the little almsmen of spring-bowers,
> Know there is richest juice in poison-flowers.
>
> (lines 97–104)

The metaphor, which asserts that the richest love is found in what is poisonous, almost hints at their identity. That is truer to the poem's sub-text than the narrator's claim for the unalloyed happiness of the opening idyll. Isabella's love is presented as being more intense in Lorenzo's absence –

> And then, instead of love, O misery!
>   She brooded o'er the luxury alone   (lines 235–6)

Although Isabella recovers from this temporary 'Selfishness' (lines 241 ff.), her emotions after recovering Lorenzo's head are those of a painfully luxurious brooding which culminates in her death. The ghost of Lorenzo, now a 'shadow' on 'the skirts of human-nature dwelling' complains that Isabella is now 'distant' from him 'in Humanity', and that he is forgetting, 'the taste of earthly bliss' (lines 305–15). His sole comfort is Isabella's paleness, foretelling her death:

> That paleness warms my grave, as though I had
> A seraph chosen from the bright abyss
> To be my spouse: thy paleness makes me glad;
> Thy beauty grows upon me, and I feel
> A greater love through all my essence steal.   (lines 316–20)

The poem claims that 'Love never dies, but lives, immortal Lord': although Love in the person of Lorenzo may be 'dead indeed', it is, says the narrator, 'not dethroned' (lines 397–400). If so the true reward of this love lies in the dead Lorenzo, 'the kernel of the grave' (line 383). Isabella, treasuring Lorenzo's rotting head whose corruption is, with the help of her tears and 'human fears', transmuted into the 'balmy' beauty of the basil plant (lines 425–32), discovers that death fulfills and absorbs her love for Lorenzo as life had not. Love in this guise is all-absorbing. The lovers' mutual loss of self in the other is a kind of self-annihilation: all else is excluded. Deprived of its object, Isabella's love centres on its loss. Her madness and death have their own logic.

Clearly, *Isabella* deals with Keats's sense of the indivisibility of joy and sorrow, beauty and pain, love and death, joyful sexuality and corruption. It is an earlier version of the 'Ode on Melancholy's 'wakeful anguish of the soul' in which 'aching Pleasure' turns 'to poison while the bee-mouth sips' (lines 10, 23–4).

Those early nineteenth-century critics who responded positively to *Isabella* thought very highly of the poem: twentieth-century critics are uneasy with it, or dismissive. It is certainly a poem which needs to be read with sympathy. Keats's difficulties in finding and maintaining as appropriate diction and tone are frequently apparent. On occasions the results are ridiculous. The repeated question 'Why were they proud?' in stanza 16 concludes feebly, 'Why in the name of Glory were they proud?' The periphrastic 'dainties' threatens to destroy the success of stanza 47, and the 'serpent's whine' of the two brothers is quite inappropriately spoken in Endymionese ('Come down . . . ere the

hot sun count/ His dewy rosary on the eglantine', lines 187–8).
The poem's description of lovers kissing has usually been
attacked:

> . . . his erstwhile timid lips grew bold,
> And poesied with hers in dewy rhyme:
> Great bliss was with them, and great happiness
> Grew, like a lusty flower in June's caress.   (lines 69–72)

Christopher Ricks's sympathetically generous reading points to
the strength of the final couplet and argues that kissing is a kind
of rhyming and vice-versa:[16] M. R. Ridley, however, found the
second line guilty of 'tasteless lusciousness' and empty of meaning.[17]

That the reader has to choose between seeing this as an
intuitively daring success or as a crass failure of taste is characteristic of the poem's verbal texture. Keats's own struggles in
arriving at a final text is evident from the help he had from others.
At least one suggestion from J. H. Reynolds was adopted into the
poem, and Richard Woodhouse not only transcribed the poem
several times, but queried passages and words, and suggested
revisions in the late summer of 1819. Taylor's opinions also
influenced the poem, and Jack Stillinger goes so far as to claim
that the help Keats received amounted to 'coauthorship'.[18] The
evidence does not allow as firm a statement as this, but it is
quite clear that a symbiotic interaction between Keats's waver-
ing uncertainties and, in particular, Woodhouse's sensibility,
which was representative of one side of contemporary taste,
produced the text as it is now known. Even its title is not that
regularly used by Keats in his letters. He always refers to *Isabella*
as 'The Pot of Basil' and to 'St Agnes Eve' rather than *The Eve
of St Agnes*.

The final published form of *The Eve of St Agnes* was without
question determined by the taste of Woodhouse and Taylor. Like
Isabella it was written quickly and unself-consciously in the period
of weightlessness following the harsh demands of a major willed
undertaking. *Isabella* had been written immediately after *Endymion*
in the early months of 1818. As *Hyperion* foundered early in 1819,
Keats turned from epic back to romance and wrote *The Eve of St
Agnes* remarkably quickly between 18 January and 2 February.

The passionate and erotic atmosphere of the poem fully taps
Keats's sensuality. In *Hyperion* he had tried to develop the serious
'speculations' which inspire one side of *Endymion*. *The Eve of St Agnes*

takes up *Endymion*'s other main concern: it is about one of the
greatest commonplace experiences, the fusion of unreasoning
desire, aching idealism, and overwhelming eroticism in youthful
love. The wide discrepancy between the very literary way in which
the subject is handled and the poem's insistence upon the
literalness of the experience are essential to the romance's success.
Like much of Keats's greatest poetry it skirts vulgarity, and is
poised precariously close to failure. The poem's world is one of
romance make-believe, highly artificial yet highly direct, a striking
union of the frank and the oblique, of knowingness and innocence,
artifice and feeling. It was precisely that delicate balance which
Keats no longer trusted when he brutally revised the poem in
September 1819, a balance kept only at the insistence of
Woodhouse and Taylor.

Formally, *The Eve of St Agnes* is a Gothic literary confection –
Keats himself drew attention to 'the fine Mother Radcliff names'
he gave to his medieval narratives. The poem is an imitation of
medieval romance, in Spenserian stanzas, dealing with a variant
of the Romeo and Juliet theme, and turns on the popular superstition that maidens who observe the proper rites on 20 January will
dream 'who shall be their first husband'.[19] However, the hero
and heroine are barely characterised, are indeed types rather than
characters, and, unlike Shakespeare's play, the story is not about
an already established mutual love. Porphyro may be at
enmity with the Baron's family and in love with Madeline, but
there is no indication in the poem that the heroine shares these
feelings until after the feast and dream episode.

The plot can easily be made to seem ominous. Porphyro comes
to the castle in secret, learns of Madeline's belief in the superstition, and persuades Angela, an old serving-woman, to conceal
him in the heroine's chamber, where he watches her undress:

> Of all its wreathed pearls her hair she frees;
> Unclasps her warmed jewels one by one;
> Loosens her fragrant bodice; by degrees
> Her rich attire creeps rustling to her knees:
> Half-hidden, like a mermaid in sea-weed,
> Pensive awhile she dreams awake (lines 227–32)

Is Porphyro, unobserved, no more than a voyeur whose excitement is meant to be shared by the reader, and are his subsequent
actions those of a ravisher rather than lover?

Recent criticism, beginning with Jack Stillinger's essay 'The

Hoodwinking of Madeline', frequently comes close to thinking so. Stillinger reads the poem as a rejection of Keats's earlier faith in 'romance' and 'fancy', and thinks the poem is ironic at the heroine's expense. Madeline's belief in the superstition is foolish and makes her dead ('amort') to the real world:

> Hoodwinked with faery fancy – all amort,
> Save to St Agnes and her lambs unshorn,
> And all the bliss to be before to-morrow morn.
>
> (lines 70–72)

Stillinger insists on the full sexuality of the bedroom scene, and points out that Angela calls Porphyro 'cruel', 'impious' and 'wicked' when he conceives his 'stratagem' (lines 139–44). Her reply after Porphyro tells her that 'This is no dream' is the traditional one of the deceived virgin:

> No dream, alas! alas! and woe is mine!
> Porphyro will leave me here to fade and pine. –
> Cruel! What traitor could thee hither bring?
> I curse not, for my heart is lost in thine,
> Though thou forsakest a deceived thing   (lines 328–32)

Madeline's 'condition is pitiful, yet at the same time reprehensible . . . as a hoodwinked dreamer she now gets her reward in coming to face reality a little too late'.[20]

The trouble with an insistently literal reading like this is that Madeline is judged far too harshly and Porphyro far too lightly. It also ignores what the poem is at pains to stress, the awe that Porphyro feels before Madeline's beauty.

> And on her hair a glory, like a saint:
> She seemed a splendid angel, newly dressed,
> Save wings, for Heaven – Porphyro grew faint;
> She knelt, so pure a thing, so free from mortal taint.
>
> (lines 222–5)

The description of the sumptuous feast of fruit –

> Of candied apple, quince, and plum, and gourd,
> With jellies soother than the creamy curd,
> And lucent syrups, tinct with cinnamon;
> Manna and dates, in argosy transferred
> From Fez; and spiced dainties, every one,
> From silken Samarkand to cedar'd Lebanon   (lines 265–70)

– which serves no function in the plot (though the feast, apparently conjured up at a moment's notice by Angela, is a symbolic lover's gift), is clearly a vehicle expressing Porphyro's sexual excitement. The fruit act as a displacement mechanism (like 'the warmed jewels') which allows Keats to include the physicality of Porphyro's desire while emphasising its curiously disembodied nature. The recurrent religious imagery serves a similar function, while the 'purple riot' in Porphyro's 'pained heart' as he conceives his stratagem (lines 136–9) is balanced by his oath to Angela that he will not 'look with ruffian passion in her face' (line 149). Missing from Stillinger's analysis is the way the lovers are, at the poem's centre, lost in one another: it describes the youthful experience of the loss of self, of identity, both in being in love and in the act of making love. Porphyro's soul, not just his body, is aching, and at that moment he is, in a manner of speaking, immortal. Madeline, waking, finds the real Porphyro 'pallid, chill, and drear' in comparison to the 'spiritual' lover of her dream, but has already fallen in love:

> 'O leave me not in this eternal woe,
> For if thou diest, my Love, I know not where to go.'

> 36
> Beyond a mortal man impassioned far
> At these voluptuous accents, he arose,
> Ethereal, flushed, and like a throbbing star
> Seen mid the sapphire heaven's deep repose;
> Into her dream he melted, as the rose
> Blendeth its odour with the violet –
> Solution sweet. Meantime the frost-wind blows
> Like Love's alarum pattering the sharp sleet
> Against the window-panes; St Agnes' moon hath set.

That contains the whole poem – the threat of the outside world set against the intense privacy of love, the simultaneously 'voluptuous' and 'ethereal' nature of Porphyro's feelings, and the marvellous tact with which the flower image, mingling smell, feel, and taste ('Solution sweet'), when coupled with his 'melting' into Madeline's dream,[21] allows the poem to speak at once on emotional and physical levels. Their coming together is a *shared* dream, but it is also a consummation. Both discover the unexpected and mysterious: both are unknowing, innocent indeed, but in differing ways. The mingling of the physical and the ideal is central to the meaning. Keats's perception, perhaps felt most strongly in youth, is that in making love we may discover that we are in love. The physical act prefigures the emotional. In that sense, a kiss between lovers is a self-fulfilling prophecy. And the dichotomy between a strong idealising drive and the force of purely erotic urgency is at no time sharper than in adolescence or early adulthood, where they are also most inextricably confused.

This is a difficult subject to talk about whether in poetry or prose. But the romance genre and the unindividuated figures of the lovers have a distancing effect. The artifice admits the special and limited nature of the experience without denying its importance. The hero and heroine, though bound by the stereotypes of romance, do fall in love. They find their true selves through their conventionalised roles. Madeline has an idea of love with no experience to match it: the romantic superstition provides her with a way to give her idealism shape. But it comes true: the dream, on this occasion, prefigures what is to happen. Her experience, while obeying a commonplace formula, is a specific and personal one discovered through Porphyro (himself conventional).

The anachronistic genre and specialised vocabulary hold off the danger of too coarsely literal a reading. For the poem to work, the reader must be divested of the self-defensive armour of irony and adult experience. The knowing and playful urbanity of Byron's *Don Juan* has no place in *The Eve of St Agnes*.

Yet Keats's alterations to the poem in September 1819 deliberately shift the poem towards the explicit. An additional stanza between 6 and 7 foretells the dream appearance of her lover, the feast he will bring, and forecasts that she will awake 'no weeping Magdalen' (that is, although she will have lost her virginity she will not regret it). The proposed conclusion was intended to 'leave on the reader a sense of pettish disgust':

> . . . Angela went off
> Twitch'd by the palsy: – and with face deform
> The Beadsman stiffen'd – 'twixt a sigh and a laugh,
> Ta'en sudden from his beads by one weak little cough.[22]

There are a number of other related changes, but the most significant was the total re-writing of the crucial stanza 36 and the two preceding lines:

> See, while she speaks his arms encroaching slow,
> Have zoned her, heart to heart, – loud, loud the dark
> winds blow!

36

For on the midnight came a tempest fell;
More sooth, for that his quick rejoinder flows
Into her burning ear: and still the spell
Unbroken guards her in serene repose.
With her wild dream he mingled, as a rose
Marrieth its odour to a violet.
Still, still she dreams, louder the frost wind blows.

Woodhouse's comments on this particular change are more revealing than is often allowed:

As the Poem was orig^y written, *we* innocent ones (ladies & myself) might very well have supposed that Porphyro, when acquainted with Madeline's love for him, & when 'he arose, Etherial flush^d &c &c . . . set himself at once to persuade her to go off with him, & succeeded & went over the 'Dartmoor black' [i.e. 'the southern moors', line 351] . . . to be married, in right honest chaste & sober wise. But, as it is now altered, as soon as M[adeline] has confessed her love, P[orphyro] instead winds by degrees his arms round her, presses breast to breast, and acts all the acts of a bonâ fide husband, while she fancies she is only playing the part of a Wife in a dream . . . and tho' there are not improper expressions but all is left to inference, and tho' profanely speaking, the Interest on the reader's imagination is greatly heightened, yet I do apprehend it will render the poem unfit for ladies, & indeed scarcely to be mentioned to them among the 'things that are'. (*Letters*, ii. 163)

While Woodhouse's bifurcated response (he prefers the 'innocent' version as literary adviser but admits that as a 'profane' man the more explicit version has a 'greatly heightened' interest) shares Taylor's conventional prejudices, he is right to say that the first version can be read innocently ('arose' *could* mean that Porphyro stands up) – as the response of nineteenth-century readers and the poem's place in school anthologies proves. More importantly, although he fails to notice that Keats's change excises Madeline's declaration of love ('For if thou diest, my love, I know not where to go'), he does note that in the new version it is unambiguously said that Porphyro makes love to Madeline while she is actually asleep ('the spell / Unbroken guards her in serene repose . . . Still, still she dreams'). In the later version, Porphyro is indeed a voyeur who has managed to transform himself into an incubus preying on Madeline.

In the text finally published, the distinction between dreaming and waking acts is altogether different. Porphyro becomes part of Madeline's 'dream of love' and instead of destroying that dream fulfils it. Natural forces (the winter sleet) act as 'Love's alarum', warning the lovers that the 'faery' period of St Agnes Eve is over: their love, that is, is endorsed by the natural world. Moreover, he regards their love as a form of marriage ('This is no dream, my bride, my Madeline!', 'sweet dreamer! lovely bride!'), and early in the story hopes that his stratagem might 'win *perhaps* that night a peerless bride' (line 167: my italics). Woodhouse's reading of the unaltered stanzas 37 to 39 (that is, the now standard text) as describing a proposal for the lovers' elopement to be followed by a marriage in 'right honest chaste and sober wise' is too pedestrian, but Porphyro, 'A famished pilgrim – saved by miracle' (line 339), *does* regard Madeline as his bride. The 'inno-cent' reading does not exclude the more literal – both take force from each other, and support the essential romance rediscovered by the poem.

Nevertheless, their love is one which cannot be satisfied in the 'be-nightmared' world of the Baron. The lovers, warned by the 'elfin-storm' –

> Hark! 'tis an elfin-storm from faery land,
> Of haggard seeming, but a boon indeed   (lines 343–4)

– escape from the drunken household, with its 'sleeping dragons all around, / At glaring watch' (lines 353–4).

> And they are gone: ay, ages long ago
> These lovers fled away into the storm.   (lines 370–71)

The storm may be benign or threatening: it is not clear. What is clear is that the castle and its inhabitants are inimical to their love.

Throughout, the poem's imagery contrasts the cold of the natural world and the heat of passion, death and life, and dream and reality. It also sets up a paradoxical relationship between religious and sensual ecstasy. *The Eve of St Agnes* begins and ends with the Beadsman:

> St Agnes' Eve – Ah, bitter chill it was!
> The owl, for all his feathers, was a-cold;
> The hare limped trembling through the frozen grass,
> And silent was the flock in woolly fold:
> Numb were the Beadsman's fingers, while he told
> His rosary, and while his frosted breath,
> Like pious incense from a censer old,

Seemed taking flight for heaven, without a death,
Past the sweet Virgin's picture, while his prayer he saith.

(lines 1–9)

The Beadsman's devotions, his suffering for 'his soul's reprieve', and his grieving 'for sinners' sake' (lines 26–7), set so sharply against the physicality of the winter animals, turns out to be more than self-mortification. His 'deathbell' has already rung as the poem opens (line 22), and his religion offers him no satisfactory answer to the coldness of death – 'his weak spirit fails' when he thinks of how 'The sculptured dead . . . may ache in icy hoods and mails' (lines 14 and 18). At the end, after the lovers have fled,

The Beadsman, after thousand aves told,
For aye unsought for slept among his ashes cold.

The Beadsman's prayers, which lead only to 'ashes', are of no service to the Baron or his warrior-guests. He is on the side of death (beadsmen were, after all, paid to pray for the dead). Porphyro and Madeline are the true pilgrims, young love the true spirituality. Even Angela, despite the help she gives Porphyro, is a 'churchyard thing' (line 155), who dies 'palsy-twitched, with meagre face deform' (line 376). The Baron's world is one of death and denial.

But the lover's 'dream' of truth insistently suggests itself as a parallel to 'Adam's dream' and hence as a paradigm of the transforming nature of the creative imagination. Indeed, the poem has been interpreted as a dramatisation of Keats's ideas about the imagination, and given a metaphysical reading. An undue emphasis on the half-hinted 'allegorical' reading disguises the delicate but tough strength of *The Eve of St Agnes*, but the poem's finely caught truth about human love is also a metaphor for the prefigurative powers of the imagination.[23]

The Eve of St Agnes, though it admits the threat to fulfilment, is a celebratory dream of love. 'La Belle Dame sans Merci' reverses that direction. The Knight's experiences hold him in 'thrall', setting him apart from the natural and human cycles of generation. Unlike *Endymion*'s moon-goddess, who is a beneficent seductress, La Belle Dame appears to the knight as seductress and destroyer. Taut, eerie, and impersonal, the ballad makes no judgements. Although 'La Belle Dame sans Merci' belongs to the Romantic cult of the ballad, evident in Bürger, Scott, Wordsworth, and Coleridge, Keats's intuitive assimilation of his sources results in a very different kind of poem.

The unyielding bareness of 'La Belle Dame sans Merci' offers no easy pointers to its psychological or metaphysical substrata. In that, it resembles its Middle English analogues. Keats's ambiguously attractive fay belongs not with the *femme fatales* who, with various names and differing psycho-sexual emphases, haunt Poe, the Pre-Raphaelites, Swinburne and Gustave Moreau, but with a more ancient tradition, that of Morgan le Fay, which lies behind Malory's *Morte D'Arthur* and Spenser's *Faerie Queene*. In this Celtic tradition the fairy goddess is paradoxically both an evil figure and a protector and nurturer of heroes, instructing them in the arts of magic and prophecy. 'La Dame du Lac, the benevolent fay, is in reality Morgan la Fée, the malevolent enchantress, in another guise, the two are part of a larger duality.'[24] Starting within a tradition of literary imitation, Keats's truth to the inner form of his story allows 'La Belle Dame sans Merci' to recreate its archetype.

The ballad gives no judgement on either the knight or the lady. Is La Belle Dame wilfully cruel to the knight? Or is it the knight's inability to sustain the vision that leads him to be cast out onto the 'cold hill side'? She has been regarded as a Circe figure, deliberately leading men to destruction through love. Robert Graves believes the ballad portrays the poet's 'Love, Death by Consumption . . . and Poetry all at once'.[25] If La Belle Dame can be identified with Keats's 'demon Poesy' she can also be seen as the obverse side of his powerful feelings for Fanny Brawne. Or the knight can be seen as being allowed to dream truth, only to awake in a withered natural world in which that truth has no place.[26] In one sense finely spun, 'La Belle Dame' is ungiving and resilient, defying paraphrase.

Nevertheless, it is clear that the 'faery' world here, as in 'Ode to a Nightingale', is at once attractive and ominous. The ballad has an antithetical relationship to the 'romance' of *The Eve of St Agnes*, and is, like the major odes, a question poem. The problematic meaning of the knight's experience, our uncertainty of the truth of his version, is the point. The knight's questioner, and hence the reader, is located firmly in the natural world of harvest and fulfilment, and is as firmly excluded from the knight's experience as he is from ours.

1

O what can ail thee, knight-at-arms,
    Alone and palely loitering?
The sedge has withered from the lake,
    And no birds sing.

2

O what can ail thee, knight-at-arms,
   So haggard and so woe-begone?
The squirrel's granary is full,
   And the harvest's done.

The knight's fairy lover, 'wild' and 'Full beautiful', looks at the knight 'as she did love', and 'in language strange she said – "I love thee true" '. But the outcome of her love is destructive:

8

She took me to her elfin grot,
   And there she wept and sighed full sore,
And there I shut her wild wild eyes
   With kisses four.

9

And there she lullèd me asleep,
   And there I dreamed – Ah! woe betide!
The latest dream I ever dreamt
   On the cold hill side.

10

I saw pale kings, and princes too,
   Pale warriors, death-pale were they all;
They cried – 'La Belle Dame sans Merci
   Thee hath in thrall!'

Whether La Belle Dame's love for the knight was feigned or true, or whether his dream was true, we cannot tell. Nor do we know whether he chooses to loiter by the withering, birdless lake, or whether his dream experience ties him there against his wish. Unlike his questioner, who lives in real time, with a past and future, the knight inhabits a wasteland more psychic than physical, and exists in a timeless present progressing towards death (an earlier but negative version of the narrator's encounter with Moneta in *The Fall of Hyperion*).

   The version of 'La Belle Dame' discussed here is that which has been printed as Keats's since 1848, drawn from the 'private' text Keats sent to the George Keatses and the one current amongst his friends. Even as a 'private' text,[27] he felt the need to add an ironic commentary (*Letters*, ii. 97):[28] this 'romance', too, Keats seems to have felt 'smokeable'. When he published the poem on 10 May 1820 in Leigh Hunt's *Indicator*, his alterations made it another poem, self-conscious and ironic. The 'knight at arms' is transformed into a 'wretched wight' – 'wight' is a conscious archaism, and the tonal change absolute: instead of sympathy, the questioner expresses impatience with the sufferer's condition:

> Ah, what can ail thee, wretched wight,
> Alone and palely loitering?

Apart from the transposition of stanzas 5 and 6, the other most important change portrays their lovemaking as mutual (in the standard version, La Belle Dame 'lulls' the knight to sleep, and so is portrayed as a seductress):

> She took me to her elfin grot,
> And there she gaz'd and sighed deep,
> And there I shut her wild sad eyes –
> So kiss'd to sleep.

> And there we slumber'd on the moss,
> And there I dream'd, ah woe betide,
> The latest dream I ever dream'd.

The 'wight' is altogether more in control than the 'knight at arms' and his lady more vapid (she gazes and sighs rather weeping and sighing 'full sore'), and the dream seems to arise from the wight's guilt at their pleasure. An element of mockery has entered the poem's treatment of its story, which is, in the *Indicator*, underlined by Keats's choice of a pseudonym, 'Caviare'.[29] *Hamlet*'s 'caviare to the general' is used to claim that Keats's poem will not be to the general taste of the time, in particular, I suspect, the kind of taste represented by his publisher Taylor who had prevented Keats from changing *The Eve of St Agnes*.[30] The creation of this partly (and half-heartedly) ironised version of 'La Belle Dame' is a further testimony, if one were needed, of Keats's inability to judge public taste.

However, the other poem Keats published in the *Indicator* includes one change which improves on the commonly accepted text, and its themes are closely related to those of the three 'medieval' narratives. On 28 May 1820 Hunt published the following poem:

A DREAM
AFTER READING DANTE'S EPISODE OF
PAOLO AND FRANCESCA.

> As Hermes once took to his feathers light,
> When lulled Argus, baffled, swoon'd and slept,
> So on a Delphic reed my idle spright
> So play'd, so charm'd, so conquer'd, so bereft

5   The dragon world of all its hundred eyes;
      And seeing it asleep, so fled away –
      Not to pure Ida with its snow-cold skies,
      Nor unto Tempe where Jove griev'd a day;
      But to that second circle of sad hell,
10   Where 'mid the gust, the world-wind, and the flaw
      Of rain and hailstones, lovers need not tell
      Their sorrows. Pale were the sweet lips I saw,
      Pale were the lips I kiss'd, and fair the form
      I floated with about that melancholy storm.

(Most modern editions omit the title, or drop its reference to Dante, essential to an understanding of the poem. All of them give 'Whirlwind', which is found in the manuscripts, instead of the *Indicator*'s coinage 'world-wind'.)[31]

Although this is not strictly a 'medieval' poem like the other three narratives, its source is Cary's translation of Dante. It was composed close in time to 'La Belle Dame', and its thematic material is clearly related to these poems. At the literal level the first six lines describe how the narrator, idly reading Dante (the 'Delphic reed'), was so wrapped up in the poem that worldly anxieties and concerns were forgotten, just as Hermes rescued Io by lulling her hundred-eyed guardian Argus to sleep with music. (He may also mean, as Miriam Allott suggests, that he stayed up late reading until the rest of the world was asleep.)[32] But the 'Delphic reed' played upon by Keats's 'idle' spirit may refer instead to Keats's own gift for poetry (for that, the opening lines must be read as part of the dream experienced by the narrator). Whichever meaning is adopted, the opposition between the inimical 'dragon-world' and that of poetry is complete. Unexpectedly, the dreaming 'spright', rather than fleeing to a beautiful poetic realm like Ida or Tempe, chooses Dante's 'second circle of sad hell'. The narrative describes a consummation of sorts, in which the dreamer ends by playing Paolo to Francesca's fair but unearthly form.

Cary's translation of Dante (1814), the one used by Keats, describes the 'torment sad' of hell's second circle to which 'carnal sinners are condemned, in whom Reason by lust is swayed' (*Hell*, v. 38–40). However, Paolo and Francesca win Dante's compassion because of their youth and innocence. Left alone reading a romance describing how love 'thralled' Lancelot, the lovers imitated the story and 'rapturously kissed' – 'The book and writer were both love's purveyors' (*Hell*, v. 122–33). Keats's lovers are not seen as 'carnal sinners'; their 'sorrows' result from the misery of the conflict between romantic love and a hostile world. Even in hell they are in the midst of the violence created by the 'world-wind', but they are at least together, with no need to explain their love. Jerome McGann comments,

when Keats emphasizes the distance between his sonnet and the original passage in Dante – when for example, he writes 'world-wind' for 'whirl-wind' and titles the sonnet 'A Dream' based on Dante – then he is telling the audience something Dante does not tell: that Dante understood the pathos of Paolo and Francesca because he was a poet, and that only poetry has the power to reach such insights.[33]

By assimilating the dreamer into Paolo's role, the poem asserts the identification of the poet with the lover, but also asserts the impossibility of poetry being able to resolve the conflict between love and reality.

The sonnet brings together into a different synthesis themes and images common to *Isabella*, *The Eve of St Agnes*, and 'La Belle Dame sans Merci'. The medieval setting or origin of all four insists on the inseparable distance between earlier poetic visions of love and modern times. 'A Dream's 'melancholy storm' and 'flaw / Of rain' are another version of the 'flaw-blown sleet' and 'elfin storm' in *The Eve of St Agnes*, while its 'pale' and 'sweet' lips, existing in an eternity of mingled torment and satisfaction, have obvious links with the 'death-pale kings' of 'La Belle Dame'. The shared concerns of these poems – the possibility or impossibility of romance, the depiction of love as rapturous or destructive thralldom, and the disturbingly close relation between love and death, grow out of the contradictory reactions to women apparent in Keats's annotations of Burton's *Anatomy*, his letters, and these poems. In all four, meaning is implicit. Unlike *Endymion*, they are not allegories. Unburdened of any need to 'explain' their significance, Keats's 'unmisgiving' imagination is free to explore the confusions created by the deep-seated struggle between his sensuality and his idealism. These four poems, taken together, are powerfully haunting realisations of the satisfactions, ambiguities, and latent destructiveness within the conception of romantic love. There is also a repeated suggestion, made most openly in the sonnet, that the ideal is one incompatible with reality.

Their resolutions also point to recurrent patterns in Keats's poetry. *The Eve of St Agnes*, like the 'Ode to Psyche', depicts human fulfilment within the fictive time that belongs to happy endings: in 'La Belle Dame' and *Lamia* a woman-figure, existing outside human time, threatens the selfhood of her mortal lover. Between these two extremes are those occasions when the speaker and a woman, who is at once benign and threatening, meet outside of time, and the narrator progresses towards knowledge, as in 'A Dream' or *The Fall of Hyperion*.

6

The spring odes, 1819

Keats's difficulties with his narrative poems were caused by his fear of an unsympathetic public and by the nature of narrative itself. The will to believe in the story told is, in Keats's narratives, threatened by the teller's awareness of its fictitiousness. Storytelling depends upon invention, and that consorted uncomfortably with Keats's insistence on truth and reality. Not only were the spring odes and the later ode 'To Autumn' written with no immediate sense of an audience, but their form gives Keats an uninhibited freedom denied him by narrative. Lyric invocation, whether of a divinity, bird, or urn, assumes that what the speaker wishes for is not a reality. Like prayer, lyric apostrophe addresses the Other in the hope that the act of speech will lead to communication between the 'I' of the poet and the presence invoked. Where a story must say 'This is so because I tell you so', an apostrophe calls for an outcome which, if wished for intensely enough, might perhaps happen. The odes' unforced quality comes not just from the spontaneity with which they were composed, but from Keats's discovery of a form which is built on the tension between what is and what might be. The very nature of the lyric ode assumes that subject and object are not one. Keats's complex urges to affirmation, questioning, and doubt are allowed full and unself-conscious play by the ode's clear distinction between speaker, object addressed, and reader. The admitted subjectivity of the genre is the basis of the odes' hard-won objectivity.

It is not at all certain that Keats himself ever realised the odes' extraordinary achievement – his belief in the primacy of the long poem and epic probably led him to under-rate these 'short' poems. Their appearance in *Lamia, Isabella, The Eve of St Agnes, and Other Poems* (1820), while giving them a degree of prominence, flattens out the radical nature of their exploratory critique of the claims of imagination and art. They are printed in a middle section called 'Poems', preceded by the three romances, and followed by *Hyperion*. That is, the romances, the first of which, *Lamia*, questions the efficacy of poetry, are followed by a set of lyrics which question but mainly affirm the powers of poetry and 'fancy'. They, in their turn, lead to a 'classical' poem presenting a vision of mankind's progressive pursuit of Beauty. The overall movement is towards an assertion of the centrality of Beauty and Truth. Yet the poems which form the middle section are an odd assortment.[1] In addition to the odes to the Nightingale, the Grecian Urn, Psyche, Autumn, and Melancholy, the vacuously nostalgic 'Lines on the Mermaid Tavern' and 'Robin Hood' are included, along with the limp ode, 'Bards of Passion and of Mirth', which celebrates the 'double immortality' of poets. Even more striking is the appearance of 'Fancy', which opens,

> Ever let the Fancy roam
> Pleasure never is at home

and concludes in the depiction of Fancy as a 'goddess' whose sexual charms outstrip those of real women. All four poems reduce the notion of poetry to the frivolously fanciful. It is as if the claims made for poetry by the volume as a whole have to be offset by a reassurance that 'poesy' is not really serious after all.

The inclusion of these weaker poems may be due to Keats's own undependable taste, that of his publisher, or the simple need to fill out pages, but they jostle against the major odes. It is a clear pointer to one side of contemporary taste that the *Eclectic Review* admired the 'pleasing and spirited numbers' of the insipid 'Fancy' while attacking the 'Ode on a Grecian Urn'. The proposition that 'Beauty is Truth' led the reviewer to comment, 'That is, all that Mr. Keats knows or cares to know. – But till he knows much more than this he will never write verses fit to live.' As the reviewer's response to 'Fancy' suggests, he really sees poetry as a form of mildly pleasurable escapism: 'Poetry, after all, if pursued as an end, is but child's play.'[2] At root, the *Eclectic Review*'s critic places no value on poetic or imaginative truth. It is a typical expression of the powerful strain of Benthamite utilitarian thinking, which saw poetry (and art) as being, at best, harmless entertainment, at worst, a form of lying. Taken as a cultural document published in July 1820, *Lamia, Isabella, The Eve of St Agnes, and Other Poems* adds up to a statement, like Hazlitt's art criticism, on behalf of the serious claims of Art and Beauty. It is a statement against the spirit of the age. Keats's earlier publication of 'Ode on a Grecian Urn' in January 1820 in *Annals of the Fine Arts*, a periodical which championed the nation's purchase of the Elgin Marbles and attacked the Royal Academy, confirms

Keats's assertion of classical and aesthetic values in opposition to prevailing taste and culture. Yet this contemporary context, which makes the 'Ode on a Grecian Urn' look like a simple affirmation of the primacy of Beauty as Truth, ignores the honesty and scepticism which lead to the profundity of the major odes. A sense of the divisions in contemporary taste helps towards an understanding of *Endymion*, and explains why Keats had such difficulties with *Isabella* and *The Eve of St Agnes*. It throws only limited light on the workings of the major odes, which hold back both from Hazlitt's whole-hearted belief in Art and Beauty and from the reductive view of poetry expressed in 'Fancy'.

Keats wrote the 'Ode to Psyche' in April 1819, shortly after giving up *Hyperion*.[3] The evolution of a satisfactory stanzaic structure for this, and the succeeding odes, grew out of Keats's experiments with the sonnet. What Keats invented was a stanza which allows thought to be developed across several stanzas without losing what Keats called the 'interwoven and complete' character of the sonnet.[4] Keats's odes strive for an interwoven completeness, returning upon their own questions, each movement cutting in a new direction, yet seeking a resolution within the original poetic premise – 'eve[r]y point of thought is the centre of an intellectual world' (*Letters*, i. 243). As a body they question one another, reformulate, and worry at closely related problems, forming a loose continued debate from the 'Ode to Psyche' to that on Indolence, with 'To Autumn' as a later and final return. Broadly speaking the odes are concerned with exclusion, with transience and loss, beauty and pain, joy and sorrow, and the challenge which experienced reality presents to the possibility of transcendence. There is a strong temptation to seek a hidden order joining them together, but each ode is separate, a spider's web growing from a specific point. They are not a developing sequence like the *Duino Elegies*, nor does Keats build up symbolic patterns like Yeats. Rather each poem feels its way from its own beginnings and in some sense returns to that beginning.

The 'Ode to Psyche' takes up once more the pastoral world of *Endymion*, and bears a strong family resemblance to the earlier Bower of Adonis (II. 387–427).[5] Both describe sleeping lovers from classical mythology, both are set in bowers, and in both the speaker comes across a vision while wandering through a forest. But there the generic similarity ends: the ode is not an episode in an allegory, but a self-contained hymn to a goddess. Keats prefaced the poem when he sent it to the George Keatses by saying –

You must recollect that Psyche was not embodied as a goddess before the time of Apulieus the Platonist who lived after [written 'aftier'] the A[u]gustan age, and consequently the goddess was never worshipped or sacrificed to with any of the ancient fervour – and perhaps never thought of in the old religion – I am more orthodox than [written 'that'] to let a hethen Goddess be so neglected – 	(*Letters*, ii. 106)

Keats's prayer to Psyche brings together *Endymion*'s bowers of imaginative and sensual fulfilment and a recurrent feature of Keats's earlier poetry, the hymn to a god. It is a 'pagan act of worship'[6] with its antecedents in the very early odes to Apollo, the 'Ode to May', and the hymns to Pan, Neptune, and Diana in *Endymion*.

But the modern poet's self-dedication as the goddess's priest in a period of unbelief starts in a dream-vision, and immediately questions its own truth:

> Surely I dreamt to-day, or did I see
> The winged Psyche with awakened eyes?	(lines 5–6)

It is the problematic status of the speaker's 'seeing' of the two sleeping lovers which provides the ode's central concern. Is the speaker's sight a 'vision' or an illusion? The opening invocation to the goddess (lines 1–4) is followed by a description of two mysterious figures which the speaker believes he has seen while wandering 'in a forest thoughtlessly'. He finally recognises the two figures sleeping in a forest bower, described in tactile images which portray the lovers' sensual satisfaction, as Cupid and Psyche (lines 5–23). Voicing his regret that Psyche, the 'latest born and loveliest vision far' of all Olympian goddesses, has no temple, rites or worshippers, the speaker undertakes, by an act of will, to become her modern hierophant:

> O brightest! though too late for antique vows,
> > Too, too late for the fond believing lyre,
> When holy were the haunted forest boughs,
> > Holy the air, the water, and the fire;
> Yet even in these days so far retired
> > From happy pieties, thy lucent fans,
> > Fluttering among the faint Olympians,
> I see, and sing, by my own eyes inspired.
> So let me be thy choir, and make a moan
> > Upon the midnight hours;
> Thy voice, thy lute, thy pipe, thy incense sweet
> > From swinged censer teeming –
> Thy shrine, thy grove, thy oracle, thy heat
> > Of pale-mouthed prophet dreaming.	(lines 36–49)

'I see, and sing, by my own eyes inspired' is an act of poetic will, and the following lines not only repeat in varied order the conclusion to the preceding stanza, where they describe the absence of Psyche's worship in modern times, but with extraordinary daring, appropriate Milton to Keats's own purposes. Milton, in 'On the Morning of Christ's Nativity', had written,

> The oracles are dumb,
> No voice or hideous hum
>   Runs through the arched roof in words deceiving.
> Apollo from his shrine
> Can no more divine
>   With hollow shriek the steep of Delphos leaving.
> No nightly trance, or breathed spell,
> Inspires the pale-eyed priest from the prophetic cell.
>
> (lines 173–80)

This is a plangent but strongly ironic account of Christ's birth displacing the superstitious paganism of classical mythology.[7] Keats transforms it first into a lament for the passing of the Olympian gods (stanza 2), and then into the bold assertion that he will recreate Psyche's worship in imaginative and inner time, denying Christian history. The paganism of the 'Ode to Psyche' is as strongly felt as that of *Endymion*, if more obviously hedged about by a refusal to claim too much.

In the final astonishing stanza, the speaker commits himself to 'building' a 'fane' for the goddess in his own mind. Although it relies on classical myth for its subject, the 'Ode to Psyche' is an attempt by the self-conscious modern imagination to create its own myth. The stanza's interiorised mental landscape, in which 'branched thoughts . . . / Instead of pines shall murmur in the wind', fledging 'the wild-ridged mountains steep by steep' (lines 52–5), seems to include and obliterate the real world.[8] Its imagined world, with 'moss-lain Dryads', 'zephyrs, streams, and birds and bees' (lines 56–7), transposes the forest setting of the first stanza into a willed and enclosed universe. In the midst of its 'wide quietness' the celebrant promises that,

> A rosy sanctuary will I dress
> With the wreathed trellis of a working brain,
>   With buds, and bells, and stars without a name,
>   With all the gardener Fancy e'er could feign,
>   Who breeding flowers, will never breed the same
>
> (lines 59–63)

Intensely felt and realised, the very concreteness of the imagery throughout the stanza could hardly contrast more sharply with the intangible workings of the mind which it describes. It is this effect perhaps which ultimately lies behind Stuart Sperry's reading of the last stanza as ironic, which he finds 'calculated' or 'rehearsed'. He goes on to argue that the poem is one concerned with the burden of modern consciousness: the poet's enshrining of the goddess in his own brain is limiting because necessarily self-conscious.[9]

The self-consciousness is certainly there, and so too an awareness of the modern speaker's isolation in celebrating the goddess. But the effect is rhapsodic and affirmatory, not ironic. Keats's choice of the words 'Fancy' and 'feign' is precise, but does not undercut the positive will of the poem. The 'Ode to Psyche' sees its myth as being at once fictive and true. Feigning is a necessary element in the workings of Fancy, but that is compensated for by the imagination's infinite multiplicity, which 'breeding flowers, will never breed the same'. Keats was indeed capable of questioning whether poetry was not a mere 'Jack a lanthern', but he also took the opposite view. The ode's 'vision' of Psyche and Cupid belongs to the realm of the 'semireal' which Keats had described in his letter of 13 March 1818 to Benjamin Bailey (the same one in which he made the 'Jack a lanthern' comment):

Things semireal such as Love, the Clouds &c which require a greeting of the Spirit to make them wholly exist – and Nothings which are made Great and dignified by an ardent pursuit – Which by the by stamps the burgundy mark upon the bottles of our Minds, insomuch as they are able to '*consec[r]ate whate'er they look upon*'.   (*Letters*, i. 243)

The 'Ode to Psyche' is the speaker's greeting of a spirit, a greeting which requires completion by the reader: both the poet and the reader 'consecrate', and so 'create', what they 'see'. The effect of the final stanza is to that of a fictive shape which awaits the coming of the goddess and her lover, a vacancy which, in Derek Walcott's words, is 'Incredulous, expecting occupancy'.[10] The conclusion awaits the return of the goddess glimpsed in the forest. 'Shadowy thought', that is, the non-consequitive thinking of the imagination grounded in sensation, can win a place for Psyche:

> And there shall be for thee all soft delight
>   That shadowy thought can win,
> A bright torch, and a casement ope at night,
>   To let the warm Love in!

Psyche, the soul, needs the completion of love, and the poem's final goal is a dream of love as well as of poetry.[11] 'The kissing and greeting of human souls' remains a theme. Poetry and human love are equally creations of the sympathetic imagination.

The 'Ode to Psyche' enacts a full circle in an upwards spiral movement. The narrator, at first doubtful of the truth of his 'vision', realises that Cupid and Psyche are homeless in an alien world. He creates a shrine for them in his own consciousness, which had itself first perceived them, or, more literally, creates their 'fane' in the act of writing the poem itself (which both perceives and creates them). The poem returns to a point just before its beginning at a higher level of perception, and awaits the completion of its reader's imagination.

The 'Ode to Psyche' has been frequently under-valued because it is the predecessor of the greater 'Ode to a Nightingale', and 'Ode on a Grecian Urn', but also because it deals openly with a classical goddess. (The 'Ode to a Nightingale' has the discretion to keep Philomel there, but in the background.) But the 'Ode to Psyche's pattern of question followed by affirmation, its banishing of doubt, make it quite distinct from the two immediately following odes.

The 'Ode on a Grecian Urn' is the most problematic of the major odes. Most recent readings have moved decisively away from the transcendentalist view, typified by Middleton Murry and Earl Wasserman, which regards Keats as fully endorsing the urn's assertion of the identity of beauty and truth – 'The intention . . . must be to uphold art as the highest form of wisdom'.[12] The urn is more generally taken as symbolic of the kind of truth proposed by art, more particularly by poetry and the imagination, but one whose order of knowing is implicitly criticised by the speaker as a limited one which denies humanity. Although intense, the figures on the urn can never consummate their desire, and belong to an ominous world of coldness and fixity.[13]

The tendency to regard the urn as a symbol for poetry or more generally, Art, obscures an essential theme, one of particular importance to the much debated final two lines. As the title (and its original appearance in *Annals of the Fine Arts*) makes clear, 'Ode on a Grecian Urn' is a meditation upon an art object, a consideration of the challenges which an art object offers the viewer. By running together the visual arts and poetry prematurely, a distinction which the poem is at pains to observe is blurred, and the ode taken outside its containing topic, the teasingly silent urn.[14]

In the first place, the ode's structure is a mimetic enactment of the viewer's experience of viewing an urn – consciously or unconsciously, the ode belongs to the long tradition, beginning with the Greeks, which attempts to transpose a picture or art object into words. With a satisfying circularity, the poem follows the eye round the urn before standing back for an overall view. Inside the leaves which surround the vase, three panels of 'leaf-fringed legend' are depicted. The first shows either men or gods pursuing the 'maidens loth' in a wild ecstasy (stanza 1), the second shows a youth, the 'Bold lover' and 'happy melodist', courting a maiden (stanzas 2–3), and the third a priest, followed by a procession, leading a heifer to sacrifice (stanza 4). The final stanza stands back, quickly recapitulates the 'brede' (that is, braid) of figures running round the urn, and ends with the urn's funerary inscription (that Keats knew the ancient use of urns to hold the ashes of the dead is clear from the 'dusty urns' in *Lamia*, II. 94).

The structure, then, creates its own poetic urn. But the interplay between literature and the plastic arts reaches from the formal to the thematic level. Time in poetry differs from time in the urn: poetry is committed to sequential time and cannot call up the instantaneously complete images round the urn, whose dimension is space. The urn's mysterious and immediate presence is unspeaking, provocative of questions ('What men or gods are these? What maidens loth?' – what or who exactly is represented remains unsaid), but yields no answers. As an art object it is fostered by 'silence and slow time' in the sense that after its maker's (that is, parent's) death, it is nurtured by the passing of the ages and kept safe from destruction, but is also nurtured by the space of silence and slow time in which the spectator apprehends an art object. 'Still unravished bride' is a double-saying. Taken as the 'bride of time', the urn is as yet unbroken by accident, or, possibly, by scholars' explications which destroy its mystery. Taken as the bride of 'quietness' the meaning seems to be that as quietness's bride (the quiet of experiencing the art-work), the urn is motionless ('still'), and both urn and quiet find their fulfilment in the exclusion of action. The lines describe the peculiar power of the urn – its instantaneity, its silent testimony, and its unanswerability to another medium, language. The division is reinforced by the admission that the urn, without effort, recreates the Arcadian 'flowery tale' which Keats had tried, ineffectually, to summon up in *Endymion* –

> Sylvan historian, who canst *thus* express
> A flowery tale more sweetly than *our rhyme*.   (my italics)

The visual arts can speak directly, if puzzlingly, across the centuries, even if the viewer is ignorant of the legend depicted or the circumstances of production.

Essential to that apparent superiority, which follows from the timeless space of the scenes depicted on the urn, is the inability to identify what is portrayed. The viewer has only minimal clues to what happens either side of the picture in time, and no indication at all whether these are gods or mortals or whether they belong geographically and historically to Tempe or Arcadia (as the latter was the favourite dwelling-place of Pan, Keats probably means to contrast a human world with one inhabited by gods).

The first stanza therefore identifies the problem. Keats longs to be the poet of timelessness and space, to create an area of knowing invulnerable to time and suffering, but the temporal nature of poetry denies that possibility. Poetry, as language, must name names and explain, and hence struggles in vain to penetrate the legend haunting the urn's 'shape'.

From this viewpoint, the urn quickly comes to seem superior not just to poetry, but to life itself – the lovers in the picture enjoy a happier love than mortals because, free of time, they will be 'For ever warm and still to be enjoyed', above 'breathing human passion' which

> . . . leaves a heart high-sorrowful and cloyed,
> A burning forehead, and a parching tongue.
>
> (lines 25–30)

In order to identify the urn's particular power for its spectator, Keats here (as throughout) defines by negatives, but that means moving out into the real world for his examples. The implicit tension between the art world and the poet's existence in time is almost ready to become an open confrontation, but not before the poet, by using a visual effect specific to poetry, that of describing what cannot be seen, triumphs over his limitations: the 'little town', 'emptied of its folk this pious morn', is inferred from the urn, and we are made to imagine the town successively and contradictorily 'by river or sea shore,/ Or mountain-built with peaceful citadel' (stanza 4).

It is the human 'desolation' of the town, whose bustling vitality is created by its absence, and which has been emptied of its folk for the timelessness of the urn, that prompts the final stanza. Although the urn still has the speaker's respect, it is seen firmly as an *objet d'art*, free of time as history or change, and so simpler than the poet's world or ours. The exclamation, 'O Attic shape! fair attitude', distances the urn to its proper sphere as aesthetic object. 'Attic' and beautiful, it remains a 'shape' not a living body, while 'attitude', whose primary meaning draws on the current art vocabulary meaning, 'The disposition of a figure in statuary or painting; hence the posture given it' (*OED*), enforces this limitation. (The modern meaning of 'attitude', that is, a 'habitual mode of regarding anything', only developed in the mid nineteenth century.) A strong note of disenchantment appears. The 'men and maidens' are 'overwrought' (that is, over-excited, as well as worked over the surface), are only 'marble', and the ironic pun on 'brede' ('braid' and 'breed') emphatically suggests the urn's exclusion from the sensual music of humanity's dying generations. Essentially still and silent, the urn 'doth tease us out of thought / As doth eternity' because eternity too is a problematic order of time, denying living experience. Hence, the 'Sylvan historian', art as sculpture or painting, turns out to be a 'Cold Pastoral', offering less than it appears to promise. Yet irony does not become bitter rejection.

> When old age shall this generation waste,
>   Thou shalt remain, in midst of other woe
> Than ours, a friend to man   (lines 46–8)

Preserved by slow time, the urn will continue to offer its silent consolation, setting its kind of time (our experience of the urn as art object) as a truth (a limited one) against process and change.

This interpretation depends upon regarding the whole of the final couplet being attributed to the urn, in the form of an admonitory inscription addressed to mankind:

>   . . . to whom thou say'st,
> 'Beauty is truth, truth beauty, – that is all
> Ye know on earth, and all ye need to know.'

(As printed in the 1820 edition, the meaning is quite different:

>   . . . to whom thou say'st,
> 'Beauty is truth, truth beauty,' – that is all
> Ye know on earth, and all ye need to know.

Here, the urn advances the general proposition, and the speaker endorses its general truth. But in Brown's transcript and in *Annals of the Fine Arts* there are no quotation marks at all, implying both lines belong to the urn, and are not necessarily supported by the speaker.[15] Even though the arrangement of the odes as printed in the 1820 volume – Nightingale, Grecian Urn, Psyche – suggests a movement from doubt to affirmation, the powerful undertow of dissatisfaction with the limitations of the Urn's world throughout the poem is such that the speaker can hardly give an unquestioning assent to the Urn's partial truth.)

In the reading adopted here axiom is followed by application. This sudden leap in linguistic levels from the dialectic of uncertainty to absolute propositional statement, can only call the urn's statement into question, making it at best a partial truth. If the urn claims too much for itself, the ode nevertheless admits the measure of consolation which it can offer. As Stuart Sperry has said very well, the urn 'is the expression of our desire to invest the intimations art affords with the permanence of certainty'.[16] Or, to use the epigraph Keats gave to the first of his two sonnets 'On Fame', written just after 'Psyche', 'You cannot eat your cake and have it too' – exactly, but human beings do want to have their cake and eat it too. The urn can offer consolation for, but not escape from, time. Neither can the urn's particular achievement be mirrored in poetry, for that must bear the burden of consciousness, the knowledge of flux and process.

Fine as it is, the 'Ode on a Grecian Urn' gives a sense of strain, of puzzling at rather than discovering its subject, as if the urn's 'teasing' objectivity hinders the seemingly inevitable modulations of the 'Ode to a Nightingale'. The Nightingale ode is the more mature and complete poem. Its tensions between flux and stasis, process and annihilation, being and non-being, are integral to structure and meaning. Means and end match perfectly. With consummate ease, the 'Nightingale' plays backwards and forwards between the spontaneous song of an actual bird and the poet's conscious and deepening reflections. Neither a goddess nor an object, the nightingale allows for an unforced meditation, an internal dialogue which is simultaneously an exchange between the human and non-human.

The ode begins and ends in real time, and is in a very profound way bound by time. Living in real time, the nightingale provides the plot by impinging upon the poet's consciousness, so provoking the reflections that make up the poem, before flying away past 'the near meadows, over the still stream,/ Up the hill-side' into 'the next valley-glades'. The poet's journey is inward towards an interior geography and history, sensed as timeless but denied by time. In the opening stanza, the listener has identified with the bird's song, as if drugged by hemlock or opiate. But the cause of this deathwards ('Lethewards') movement is an overwhelming happiness so intense as to be painful. The 'drowsy numbness' which pains his sense is ecstatic and springs not from envy of the bird, but from 'being too happy in thine happiness'. Sympathetic identification has led almost to an obliteration of selfhood. The second stanza expresses a yearning to become one with the bird's world – 'O, for a draught of vintage', that the mind dispossessed by alcohol might let the poet 'fade away into the forest dim', and 'leave the world unseen' (both unseen by the world and unable to see the world). The enemy, as stanza 3 makes clear, is the 'weariness, the fever, and the fret/ Here, where men sit and hear each other groan', and where Beauty and Love are transient. Faced with this reality, drugs or drink are an evasion.

In the next movement of the ode, the poet, through a willed decision, determines to join the bird through the human equivalent of its song, 'the viewless wing of Poesy'. Briefly, he attains that realm ('Already with thee'), and reaches a state of pure sensation (characteristically imaged through images of touch, taste, and smell) which surpasses the 'dull brain' –

> I cannot see what flowers are at my feet,
>   Nor what soft incense hangs upon the boughs,
> But in embalmed darkness, guess each sweet
>   Wherewith the seasonable month endows
> The grass, the thicket, and the fruit-tree wild –
>   White hawthorn, and the pastoral eglantine
>
> (lines 41–6)

Endymion's luxuriant bowers of interwreathed senses and total satisfaction are metamorphosed into an ominously attractive psychological urge. 'Embalmed' points up the movement towards a more final kind of nothingness than that of the first stanza, the total loss of consciousness. Stanza 6 makes that direction explicit, but at the cost of the speaker returning to awareness of the self:

> Darkling I listen; and, for many a time
>   I have been half in love with easeful Death,
> Called him soft names in many a mused rhyme,
>   To take into the air my quiet breath

But the poet is strictly only half in love with easeful death, it only *seems* rich to die. The bird would sing, but the poet would 'have ears in vain – / To thy high requiem become a sod'.

Bird and poet then are separate, and the penultimate stanza, reaching back through human recorded history, sings of the 'immortality' of the nightingale's song, and its continuing power to affect the imagination, to charm –

> . . . magic casements, opening on the foam
> Of perilous seas, in faery lands forlorn.

The bird does live through its song's effect on endless human listeners. But 'forlorn', which appears in the archaising and alliterative compound 'faery lands forlorn' merely as a weakened poeticism for 'desolate', begins the final movement with substantial irony –

> Forlorn! the very word is like a bell
> To toll me back from thee to my sole self!

(lines 71–2)

Here it has taken on the sense of 'Forsaken by (a person); bereft, destitute, or stripped of (a thing)' (*OED*). Geoffrey Hill comments:

The echo is not so much a recollection as a revocation; and what is revoked is an attitude towards art and with art. The menace that is flinched from is certainly mortality ('Where youth grows pale and spectre-thin, and dies') but it is also the menace of the high claims of poetry itself. 'Faery lands forlorn' reads like an exquisite pastiche of a Miltonic cadence: 'Stygian caves forlorn' ('L'Allegro', line 3); 'these wilde Woods forlorn' (*Paradise Lost*, ix. 910).[17]

Tolled disturbingly back from reverie to self-awareness and self knowledge, the poet is deserted by the nightingale both literally and metaphorically. Poetry, the imagination (which, tellingly, Keats terms 'Fancy'), 'cannot cheat so well/ As she is famed to do, deceiving elf' – poetry is a faery temptress. And the ode ends in uncertainty and doubt –

> Was it a vision, or a waking dream?
> Fled is that music – Do I wake or sleep?

Keats yearns to attain the pure being of the natural world, in which the nightingale's 'full-throated ease' appears a perfect equivalent for human song (lyric poetry). Yet the equivalence only reveals the limitations. Human consciousness inalienably excludes man from the un-thinking, non-conscious utterance of the nightingale. For the poet, agonisingly aware of the undifferentiating destructiveness of chronological time, the bird's song becomes the type of a poetry whose time scale would be of another order, seeking to fix in words those moments of significant time

– what Wordsworth had called 'spots of time', Joyce was to name
'epiphanies' and which Virginia Woolf called 'moments of Being'
– those rare ecstatic moments when consciousness loses its sense
of self, and the ego is overwhelmed by visionary being, freed from
clock-time. The paradox of the poem is that by admitting failure
it, as if inadvertently, demonstrates the grandeurs of the human
singer, who, within his own limits, gives the bird immortality –
an immortality that exists only in the human mind. The
nightingale is never seen in the ode, only heard, and then only
through the poet's words, yet the bird's meaning to humanity,
and in that sense its song, is recreated. Poetry, since it recreates
that other order of time for each subsequent reader, also defies
chronological time.

For the common reader, Keats's suspicion of the authenticity or
sufficiency of art as a reply to our direct knowledge of suffering
and the imperfections of time, has a convincing sanity. Although
dealing with the same crux as Wallace Stevens, he cannot manage
the twentieth-century poet's confidence in art which places the
imagination at the centre of man's transformation of the universe
into meaningfulness –

> A tune beyond us as we are,
> Yet nothing changed by the blue guitar;
>
> Ourselves in the tune as if in space,
> Yet nothing changed, except the place
>
> Of things as they are and only the place
> As you play them, on the blue guitar,
>
> Placed, so, beyond the compass of change,
> Perceived in a final atmosphere;
>
> For a moment final, in the way
> The thinking of art seems final when
>
> The thinking of god is smoky dew.
> The tune is space. The blue guitar
>
> Becomes the place of things as they are,
> A composing of senses of the guitar.
>
> (*The Man with the Blue Guitar*, vi)

Nor can Keats move towards Wordsworth's elated affirmations of
the transforming powers of the imagination's perception of
nature:

> . . . Therefore am I still
> A lover of the meadows and the woods
> And mountains; and of all that we behold
> From this green earth; of all the mighty world
> Of eye and ear – both what they half create,
> And what perceive; well pleased to recognise
> In nature and the language of the sense
> And anchor of my purest thoughts, the nurse,
> The guide, the guardian of my heart, and soul
> Of all my moral being.   ('Tintern Abbey', lines 102–11)

Stevens, with a surety that nearly resembles complacency when set against Wordsworth's prolonged meditations, similarly pursues a 'poem of the mind'. Within his own terms, Keats takes up at the point when Wordsworth turns from the world of man to that of nature. Felt experience (and common experience) is, paradoxically, where Keats, ostensibly a poet of sight, finds his ground. 'Scenery is fine – but human nature is finer'.[18] The odes, like Keats's other major poems, are not about landscape, but about figures and people, and are concerned with how it feels to be puzzled and pained, yet joyful and ecstatic. If Wordsworth's poetry is above all sustained by 'joy', Keats's essential experience is the oxymoronic realisation that pain is indivisible from joy.

That paradox receives its most memorable formulation in the 'Ode on Melancholy':

> She dwells with Beauty – Beauty that must die;
>   And Joy, whose hand is ever at his lips
> Bidding adieu; and aching Pleasure nigh,
>   Turning to poison while the bee-mouth sips:
> Ay, in the very temple of Delight
>   Veiled Melancholy has her sorvran shrine,
>   Though seen of none save him whose strenuous tongue
> Can burst Joy's grape against his palate fine.   (lines 21–8)

Beauty, joy and 'aching Pleasure' exist only in time. But the point is not that their transience makes for mere poignancy. Except in time, beauty and joy, here imaged in powerfully sexual terms, have no human meaning. Only those self-conscious enough to 'burst Joy's grape' will recognise that pure joy is defined by its absence. Hence Melancholy's 'sovran shrine' (that is, her true and efficacious as well as imperial shrine) is hidden in the 'very temple of Delight'. Or as Wallace Stevens put it – 'Death is the mother of beauty.' 'Sunday Morning', however, speaks with a gravity and a near-proselytising conviction, where Keats's ode, for all its grandiloquence, takes itself with less seriousness.

The ode is an imperfectly achieved poem, but an interesting one. It will not do to regard 'Melancholy' either too solemnly or as an obvious example of decadent self-indulgence. Nevertheless, critics like F. R. Leavis and Douglas Bush who are worried by an apparent aestheticism, though they undervalue the poem's self-awareness, do single out something important, the element of attitudinizing. Keats, in fact, begins by attacking the posturings of a false melancholy. The opening stanza is a wittily ironic rejection of a sentimental contemplation of suicide.

> No, no, go not to Lethe, neither twist
> Wolf's-bane, tight-rooted, for its poisonous wine . . .
> For shade to shade will come too drowsily,
> And drown the wakeful anguish of the soul.

That is, if you want the full experience of melancholy, it is a mistake to seek suicide, for the shady truths of melancholy rely on the 'wakeful anguish of the soul', which are drowned in the all too final shades of death. You will become a ghost (exactly the wrong kind of 'shade'). Empson describes the tone as that of well-meant avuncular advice, and also points out that the negatives ('No, no') presuppose a strong urge towards this kind of self-obliteration on the part of both reader and poet.[19] The note of deliberate comedy implies a distance from the topic, and is a reminder that the ode is on, not to, Melancholy.

The second stanza defines Melancholy as involuntary not self-induced. In this form it is at once creative and touched by death. The honorific identification of Melancholy with the April rains which 'shroud' the 'green hills' yet 'foster' the flowers, which themselves mourn because 'droop-headed', brilliantly implies its generative powers. 'Sorrow' should be 'glutted' on images of transience, on the 'wealth of globed peonies'. Keats's stance is that of an experienced mentor. Having rejected the self-regarding excess of stanza 1, this middle section represents the right response. Overwhelmed by unwilled melancholy, he advises that we experience it to the fullest, yet the final lines seem themselves to strike an attitude –

> Or if thy mistress some rich anger shows,
> Emprison her soft hand, and let her rave,
> And feed deep, deep upon her peerless eyes.

(lines 18–20)

This is the crux. The lines invite the charge of callous, even sadistic, indifference to the mistress's feelings. In defence it has been argued that this is an example of Keatsian intensity. The lover responds to the vital fullness of being apparent in someone wholly given over to anger, and the disagreeables evaporate in the act of contemplation. All the same, as practical advice it is difficult to act upon and likely to lead to a rightfully indignant reply. A rather more satisfactory explanation is that the next stanza resolves the problem since the mistress addressed there ('She dwells with Beauty') is clearly the goddess Melancholy. Focused back on the earlier lines, the mistress is to be seen as both an actual mistress and the goddess. While this syntactical ambiguity helps some of the way, it does not altogether answer the original objection and raises another. Ought a lover allow his mistress to rave while he feeds on her eyes? Is it in character for the goddess Melancholy to lose her temper and 'rave' at her devotee? The human and fictive levels do not satisfactorily support one another. It might be better to take the concluding lines of the second stanza with the third, and allow an ironic dimension to the handling of Melancholy's devotee there. 'None save him' can perceive Melancholy in the temple of Delight, but equally he is finally hung up as one of Melancholy's 'cloudy trophies'. Certainly the feel of the verse suggests that Keats entertains rather than endorses the ideas expressed.

Nevertheless, the possibility that Keats was in less than full control of his material cannot be ruled out. There is a revealing difficulty in the lines –

> . . . and aching Pleasure nigh,
> Turning to poison while the bee-mouth sips.

> (lines 23–4)

Even if the awkwardness of the personification 'Pleasure' turning into poison is overcome, there is still the question of whether the 'bee-mouth' belongs to Pleasure, Melancholy, or the lover (all seem possible grammatically). This does not seem to be a fruitful ambiguity. Yet when reading the poem, the extraordinary truth through feel of the sipping bee-mouth allows the reader to slip past the awkwardness, suggests that the strength lies elsewhere, in the way the ode isolates those moments caught between one state and the next –

> And Joy, whose hand is ever at his lips
> Bidding adieu . . .

The oddity of diction, the near preciousness of 'Bidding adieu', and the catching of a gesture, are a characteristic Keatsian triumph. Personification takes on a new kind of life, gestural rather than static, the emotion felt and experienced rather than intellectual and abstract. The idea is of the intensity of joy being dependent upon a sense of its passing. As soon as we know that we are experiencing joy, it has begun to decay. Or to put it another way, this anguished wakeful parting with Joy is complementary to Keats's yearning to reach the world of pure poetry, the ideal. They are twin aspects of Keats's sense of exclusion, of alienation, from pure being, but are here recognised as integral to knowledge. Knowledge brings sorrow, so in a sense sorrow is knowledge and beauty is sorrow.

The limitations of the 'Ode on Melancholy' point to a recurrent problem in Keats, and are most clearly seen by relating its theme to its source in Burton's *Anatomy of Melancholy*. 'La Belle Dame', *Lamia* and 'Melancholy' all owe something to the *Anatomy*, and what is owed goes beyond verbal resemblances. At some level, Burton acted as a catalyst for the formulation of Keats's less conscious attitudes to sexuality, his unease and anxieties. To that extent, these poems are a true tribute to Burton's treatise on love melancholy. In the case of the 'Ode on Melancholy', Burton limits as well as propels Keats's imagination. The *Anatomy*, for all its eccentric vigour and, for Keats, antique flavour, is rationalist, factual and humanist in both structure and intention. Its logical divisions and subdivisions signal a way of thinking profoundly opposed to the symbolic meaning given Melancholy in the pictorial tradition of the Italian Renaissance. There, as Panofsky has demonstrated,[20] the identification of Melancholy with Saturn anticipates romanticism in aligning the isolated, suffering melancholic, threatened by madness, with the creativity of genius. Dürer's figure of Melancholia, surrounded by the symbols of knowledge and craft, is the best-known representation of this ambiguous figure. Burton's humane insistence upon the physiological and psychological causes of melancholy (that is, depression), places him outside that tradition. His robust commonsense casts him as a humane materialist answering the metaphysical and symbolic speculations of Renaissance syncretic thought. However, as she appears in Keats's ode, Melancholy is an attenuated and literary figure, related to those eighteenth-century descendants of Milton's 'Il Penseroso' such as Thomas Warton's *Pleasures of Melancholy*. Where 'La Belle Dame sans

Merci' reaches behind the literary fashion for the ballad towards an archetypal source, in the ode Keats cannot get sufficiently beyond the personification to put his goddess in touch with the full power of the older conception of Melancholy. The ode circles the edges of this idea rather than inhabiting it. Critics find the poem puzzling because they rightly sense the profundity and seriousness of its theme and its centrality to Keats. Linked to the letters and other poems, a sense of the whole can be displayed. But that area of knowing is something that does not quite get into the poem.

The odes' 'speculations' spring spontaneously from a mood at once questioning and receptive. With a sudden impatience, the 'Ode on Indolence' rejects the state of negative capability out of which the odes grew, characterising the whole effort of the odes as worthless. Traditionally dated as the last of the spring odes,[21] 'Melancholy' is openly escapist:

> O, for an age so sheltered from annoy,
> That I may never know how change the moons,
>   Or hear the voice of busy common-sense!

(lines 38–40)

The ode recalls the themes of the major odes, but does so only to dismiss them. For both the poet and reader there is a strong sense of *déjà vu*, troubling rather than enabling. Three mysterious figures appear to the speaker, 'like figures on a marble urn' (line 5). They are later identified:

> The first was a fair Maid, and Love her name;
> The second was Ambition, pale of cheek,
>   And ever watchful with fatigued eye;
> The last, whom I love more, the more of blame
> Is heaped upon her, maiden most unmeek –
>   I knew to be my demon Poesy.   (lines 25–30)

All three are wished away in favour of a luxuriously idle 'summer-indolence'. The ode's final assertion that even without Love, Ambition, or the 'demon Poesy' the narrator still has sufficient 'visions for the night' and 'faint visions for the day' (lines 57–9), is unconvincing and completely unsupported. This final spring ode can only be read as a total, if temporary, rejection of the importunate and self-aggrandising claims of poetry. On 9 June Keats wrote to Sarah Jeffrey, berating the English public for its repeated failure to recognise great poets during their lifetime, and went on to say:

I have been very idle lately, very averse to writing; both from the over-powering idea of our dead poets and from abatement of my love of fame. I hope I am a little more of a Philosopher than I was, consequently a little less of a versifying Pet-lamb.   (*Letters*, ii. 173)

In the ode, Keats's belief that knowledge is essential to the writing of great poetry, lies behind his scornful dismissal of contemporary poetic fame:

> So, ye three ghosts, adieu! Ye cannot raise
>   My head cool-bedded in the flowery grass;
> For I would not be dieted with praise,
>   A pet-lamb in a sentimental farce!   (lines 51–4)

The origins of this outburst are identical with Keats's reasons later in the year for wishing to alter *The Eve of St Agnes*: fashionable success was, he believed, entirely dependent upon satisfying a demand for sentimentality.

The fear that he would never achieve his ambitions, allied to a sense of the greatness of his predecessors, ultimately lies behind the ode's wish for 'nothingness' (line 20). That same complex of feelings about love, poetry, fame, and nothingness comes together powerfully in an earlier sonnet:

> When I have fears that I may cease to be
>   Before my pen has gleaned my teeming brain,
> Before high-piled books, in charactery,
>   Hold like rich garners the full-ripened grain;
> When I behold, upon the night's starred face,
>   Huge cloudy symbols of a high romance,
> And think that I may never live to trace
>   Their shadows, with the magic hand of chance;
> And when I feel, fair creature of an hour!
>   That I shall never look upon thee more,
> Never have relish in the faery power
>   Of unreflecting love! – then on the shore
> Of the wide world I stand alone, and think
> Till love and fame to nothingness do sink.

This extraordinary expression of mingled ardour, humility, and yearning, and its open admission of Keats's innermost feelings, make the sonnet a semi-private poem (it was only published after his death). The 'Ode on Indolence' is an unsuccessfully realised and private poem. When he came to write the ode, the Keats of *Hyperion*, the poet who wished to do some good in the world, cast aside the spring odes as indulgent self-deceptions. Although

Keats, like Yeats, is a poet whose growth and development follows a pattern of self-renewal based on an argument with his earlier work, the 'Ode on Indolence's mockery of the spring odes has an ironic pathos. Keats died regretting that he had left nothing to posterity worthy of his genius, unable to recognise the pre-eminence of the major odes.

7

Final poems

The crisis of will in early summer 1819 was followed by a fresh commitment to poetry. On 17 June Keats told his sister that he had been preparing to 'enqu[i]re for a Situation with an Apothecary' but that Charles Brown had persuaded him 'to try the press once more' (*Letters*, ii. 121). Less than a month later he was hard at work, in retreat on the Isle of Wight. He wrote to Reynolds, 'I have great hopes of success, because I make use of my Judgment more deliberately than I yet have done; but in Case of failure with the world, I shall find my content' (*Letters*, ii. 128). Keats had begun a period of astonishing creativity. Between June and the end of 1819, he had written *Lamia*, rewritten *Hyperion* as *The Fall of Hyperion*, completed a five-act drama, *Otho the Great*, with Charles Brown and started another, as well as writing nearly 800 lines of an unfinished satire, 'The Cap and Bells, or, The Jealousies'. In addition, he wrote 'To Autumn', a number of shorter lyric poems, and revised *The Eve of St Agnes*.

Writing 'deliberately' and trying to meet what he saw as the public's taste, were of dubious advantage to the 'unmisgiving' side of Keats's sensibility. In the case of the tragedy which he wrote jointly with Brown while simultaneously composing *Lamia* and *The Fall of Hyperion*, this did not matter: the play was intended as a vehicle for the talents of the actor Edmund Kean and did not draw deeply on Keats's imagination. The effects of deliberation and judgement on *Lamia* are another matter. Its tone and feel are quite unlike any other of Keats's poems. It is cold, bright, distanced from, and, on crucial occasions, self-conscious about, its very Keatsian subject matter.

The awkwardness was intended, and explains Keats's particular fondness for the poem. *Lamia* had, he believed, 'that sort of fire in it which must take hold of people in some way – give them either pleasant or unpleasant sensation' (*Letters*, ii. 189). The effect aimed at is to shock the expectations of 'mawkish' readers of romance and to measure up to the taste of those with 'knowledge of the world'.

The result is unsettled and unsettling. While the story is told from a point of view predominantly sympathetic to Lamia, the narrator's slanting of the tale and occasional eruptions into the text demand another response. The reader is asked to sympathise with Lamia's other-world beauty and with the piteousness of her story, but is also expected to recognise her fictitiousness and untruth. In the earlier part of the poem in particular the distancing works well. Elsewhere there is a crippling conflict between the call for sympathy and the narrator's desire to cut things down to 'worldly' size. Intended as a critique of the reader's 'romantic' expectations, *Lamia* opens up, and appears to endorse, an unbridgeable chasm between the pleasures of fancy and the realities of life, between earlier poetic fictions and modern reality, and between the conventional idealisation of 'Love' and the disillusion of mature experience. This kind of polarisation, and its accompanying explicitness, denies the kind of truthfulness attained by the 'unmisgiving' version of *The Eve of St Agnes*. It is also the cause of the widely different readings and assessments of the poem.

Keats took his plot from Burton's *Anatomy of Melancholy*. There it is a story of how Lycius, a young student of Corinth, is saved by his teacher Apollonius from his love for and marriage to a lamia, a serpent in woman's guise. Burton cites the matter-of-fact tale from Philostratus as proof from classical sources for the existence of Satanic incubi and succubi. Keats's reworking adds an introductory episode showing Lamia's transformation into human form, develops the characters of Lamia and Lycius, and makes Apollonius' intervention the cause of Lycius' death. Lamia, then, is a Romantic archetype, the demon-lover. She is simultaneously attractive and threatening, and represents both the female principle, and the 'romance' imagination.

The poem's opening is marvellously assured. Keats's recent study of Dryden and the influence of Marlowe's *Hero and Leander* appear in the tightened couplets and ironic distancing from the mythological material. The first lines create an alliance of near-pastiche and poignancy:

> Upon a time, before the faery broods
> Drove Nymph and Satyr from the prosperous woods,
> Before King Oberon's bright diadem,
> Sceptre, and mantle, clasped with dewy gem,
> Frighted away the Dryads and the Fauns
> From rushes green, and brakes, and cowslipped lawns,

> The ever-smitten Hermes empty left
> His golden throne, bent warm on amorous theft.

The 'ever-smitten Hermes', only too susceptible to the charms of mortal nymphs, is touched by comedy, just as the 'rushes green, and brakes, and cowslipped lawns', with their Elizabethan lushness, are at once literary and moving. The once-upon-a-time opening locates the reader in a fictional time past. Very deftly, Keats transports us back through the ahistorical era of Shakespeare's 'faery broods' to the mythological period of classical nymphs and satyrs in ancient Crete. By making the Greek Hermes the immediate predecessor of Oberon's fairy world, Keats links pagan mythology to an English 'myth', giving both fresh vitality, but equally placing both worlds as literary fictions. They are worlds lost to the modern reader or narrator. Hermes, in love with his Cretan nymph, is both more and less than human. The god is flushed with excitement at the thought of the nymph –

> . . . a celestial heat
> Burnt from his winged heels to either ear,
> That from a whiteness, as the lily clear,
> Blushed into roses 'mid his golden hair,
> Fallen in jealous curls about his shoulders bare (I. 22–26)

– and is subject to the comic absurdities of jealousy (he is 'full of painful jealousies/ Of the Wood-Gods, and even the very trees' (I. 33–34). Unlike humans, however, he is secure because the serpent-enchantress Lamia, potent in her own world, enables him to find and enjoy the nymph. It is an attractive but non-human world, whose simplicities and satisfactions call for irony when set against human experience.

Once Keats has established this ironic frame, the beauty of Lamia in her serpent form can be described without irony, and the 'gentle heart', hearing her 'mournful voice', can feel only 'pity' (I. 35–7).

> She was a gordian shape of dazzling hue,
> Vermilion-spotted, golden, green, and blue;
> Striped like a zebra, freckled like a pard,
> Eyed like peacock, and all crimson barred;
> And full of silver moons, that, as she breathed,
> Dissolved, or brighter shone, or interwreathed
> Their lustres with the gloomier tapestries –
> So rainbow-sided, touched with miseries,

> She seemed, at once, some penanced lady elf,
> Some demon's mistress, or the demon's self.   (I. 47–56)

Her strange beauty, drawing on natural and animal images, and verging on the grotesque, is disturbing as well as attractive. (The passage is an example of the distinction Keats draws between Byron and himself, 'He describes what he sees – I describe what I imagine – Mine is the hardest task' (*Letters*, ii. 200).) Lamia has previously been a woman and wants a 'woman's shape' as 'charming as before' (I. 118). Her transformation into a human from 'elfin' shape is threatening as well as painful. The foam from her mouth is 'so sweet and virulent' that it withers the grass, and her metamorphosis is described in images of phosphoric fire and volcanic violence, which destroy her serpent's beauty (I. 146–68). Only the reader sees this transformation (when she dies, she simply vanishes from Lycius' arms – to become a lamia again?). We, then, know her agony, but it is important that in the space between Lamia's putting off the snake's form and assuming human shape, 'Nothing but pain and ugliness were left' (I. 164). The poem hints that Lamia's beauty conceals only ugly pain. This, taken with the narrator's calling her a 'paramour' (II. 83) and naming her house as 'That purple-lined palace of sweet sin' (II. 31), seem to identify Lamia's sexuality with an unwittingly destructive power.

But if she appears like a 'demon's mistress, or the demon's self', she also seems to Hermes 'surely high inspired' (I. 83), and there is a firm suggestion that she represents a form of the imagination. She has the power while in her 'serpent-prison house' to send her spirit wherever she wills in the human and Olympian realms. She foreknows Hermes' errand (I. 68–79), and falls in love with Lycius when she sends 'Her dream' to Corinth (I. 213–19). One reading, then, is that Lamia is an 'elf-demon-faery', and that 'Lycius is destroyed by a cheat'. Lamia, according to W. H. Evert, represents 'Keats's revised view of the poetic imagination' her 'beauty is false and her effect on human life pernicious.' Not only does she represent the effects of the poetic imagination on Lycius, but she is herself a victim of imagination. Only brief participation in the world is possible before she is destroyed by reality.[1]

This reading, though partial because it minimises Lamia's sexuality, gives coherence to much of the poem as a criticism of the limits of fancy. Keats breaks the poem at the end of Part I, when Lamia has met and gained Lycius' love, and addresses the reader directly:

> And but the flitter-winged verse must tell,
> For truth's sake, what woe afterwards befell,
> 'Twould humour many a heart to leave them thus,
> Shut from the busy world, or more incredulous.   (I. 394–7)

That is, many readers would like the story to conclude at this point, 'incredulous' that anything could happen to disturb the happy ending. But a poetry faithful to reality must go on to tell the painful ending. The use of 'many' and the rejected couplet –

> But now is Poesy's long ember week
> And against fashion, folly 'tis to sin

– indicate that Keats saw himself as challenging the majority's preference for the untrue endings of romance as against the reality of life. Part II represents as it were, the 'true' continuation of *The Eve of St Agnes*, and Lamia is the false 'demon Poesy' of fancy.

The poem is therefore about mutually exclusive categories of perception, and Lamia's doomed attempt to cross their boundaries. Hermes, who successfully crosses from the Olympian to the pastoral world in pursuit of his nymph, provides a comic parallel to Lamia's fatal passage into the 'busy' human world of Corinth. Lamia's longings and Apollonius' philosophy are irreconcilable.

> . . . Do not all charms fly
> At the mere touch of cold philosophy?
> There was an awful rainbow once in heaven:
> We know her woof, her texture; she is given
> In the dull catalogue of common things.
> Philosophy will clip an Angel's wings,
> Conquer all mysteries by rule and line,
> Empty the haunted air, and gnomed mine –
> Unweave a rainbow, as it erewhile made
> The tender-personed Lamia melt into a shade.
>
> (II. 229–38)

The reader is directed to feel sympathy for the lovers, as the wreaths imagined for the three main characters make clear. Lamia's 'willow' and 'adder's tongue' symbolise grief and sorrow, while the ivy and vineleaves stripped from Bacchus' thyrsus for Lycius are to stop him seeing Apollonius' discovery of Lamia. The wreath for Apollonius –

> Let spear-grass, and the spiteful thistle wage
> War on his temples.   (II. 228–9)

123

– show that the narrator and reader should sympathise with Lycius' outburst against Apollonius' 'juggling eyes' and his 'impious proud-heart sophistries' (II. 277, 285). If Apollonius' stern insistence on seeing things for what they are (Lamia is a serpent really, that and no more) alienates the reader, the poem castigates Lycius as 'senseless' and a 'Madman' for making his love public (II. 147) despite Lamia's warning. Nevertheless, Apollonius' philosophy does destroy the lovers: modern rationalism denies the truth of poetry as represented by Lamia. *Lamia*'s scepticism may be limited only to the poetry of 'fancy', the poetry of the mere 'dreamer', but unlike *The Fall of Hyperion*, it gives no sign that there is any other kind, nor that philosophy can be anything but reductive. The opposition is too simplistic, one which Leigh Hunt rightly called 'a common-place', 'a condescension to a learned vulgarism'.[2]

Lamia, however, is not just about the opposition between poetry and scientific rationalism, though Hunt and nineteenth-century criticism saw the poem in this way. It is also about the antagonism between love and everyday life, which is here, as in the sonnet on Paolo and Francesca, taken to be total. Even though Cupid takes particular care of the two lovers, their love will be 'ruined' –

> Love, jealous grown of so complete a pair,
> Hovered and buzzed his wings, with fearful roar,
> Above the lintel of their chamber door,
> And down the passage cast a glow upon the floor.

> For all this came a ruin . . .   (II. 12–16)

The image is meant to be of Love jealously guarding the completeness of their love against intrusion, though the awkward phrasing almost suggests the opposite – that Cupid is violently jealous *of* their love's perfection. What destroys them is Lycius' inability to remain satisfied with endless sensual satisfaction. As soon as any thought of the outside world enters his mind, their love is doomed:

> His spirit passed beyond its golden bourne
> Into the noisy world almost forsworn.
> The lady, ever watchful, penetrant,
> Saw this with pain, so arguing a want
> Of something more, more than her empery
> Of joys; and she began to moan and sigh
> Because he mused beyond her, knowing well
> That but a moment's thought is passion's passing-bell.

> (II. 32–39)

'Thought' destroys passion as well as poetry: their love can only exist as long as it is private, and as long as Lycius is wholly absorbed in Lamia's 'empery/ Of joys'. While this inimical opposition of the busy and rational world to Lamia's love for Lycius is a matter for pity at the end of the poem, the narrator opens Book II with an attempt at jocular irony:

> Love in a hut, with water and a crust,
> Is – Love, forgive us! – cinders, ashes, dust;
> Love in a palace is perhaps at last
> More grievous torment than a hermit's fast.

Love, even love in a 'purple-lined palace of sweet sin', does not last. In the human world love inevitably turns to bitterness –

> . . . but too short was their bliss
> To breed distrust and hate, that make the soft voice hiss.
>
> (II. 9–10)

Keats's 'knowledge of the world' turns out to be coarse-grained. The same coarseness appears in the narrator's earlier assertion that real women are preferable to poetic fictions:

> Let the mad poets say whate'er they please
> Of the sweets of Faeries, Peris, Goddesses,
> There is not such a treat among them all,
> Haunters of cavern, lake, and waterfall,
> As a real woman, lineal indeed
> From Pyrrha's pebbles or old Adam's seed. (I. 328–333)

The reduction of women to sweet 'treats' speaks for an imperciply commonplace view of women's submissive sexual role.

Keats's effort to portray the lovers' relationship in greater psychological depth than in his earlier romances is similarly flawed. When Lycius decides to make their love public, he explains his reasons:

> 'What mortal hath a prize, that other men
> May be confounded and abashed withal,
> But lets it sometimes pace abroad majestical . . .
> Let my foes choke, and my friends shout afar,
> While through the thronged streets your bridal car
> Wheels round its dazzling spokes.' (II. 57–64)

The motivation is as crude as it is unconvincing (quite apart from the fact that there is no sign that Lycius has any enemies). Determined to persuade her to his will, Lycius' passion turns to cruelty:

JOHN KEATS

Perverse, with stronger fancy to reclaim
Her wild and timid nature to his aim:
Besides, for all his love, in self-despite,
Against his better self, he took delight
Luxurious in her sorrows, soft and new.
His passion, cruel grown, took on a hue
Fierce and sanguineous   (II. 70–76)

Although Lycius' aggression is described as 'perverse', Lamia
responds:

   . . . She burnt, she loved the tyranny,
And, all subdued, consented to the hour   (II. 81–82)

Keats's comment on this passage – 'Women love to be forced
to do a thing, by a fine fellow – *such as this*' (*Letters*, ii. 164) –
only enforces the ugliness of one level of feeling moving behind
Lamia's surface. The obverse of 'sweet pain' is violence and
domination, whether of the woman by the man or the man by the
woman.

Neither Taylor nor Woodhouse, who worked carefully through
the whole text, seem to have had any objection to this passage, nor
did contemporary critics. The reviewer in *The British Critic*, on the
watch for any detail which might 'wound delicacy', says only that
Burton's story is 'a very agreeable fiction' which 'loses none of its
merit in the hands of Mr. Keats.'[3] This silence can only mean
that Woodhouse, Taylor, and the reviewer thought the passage
acceptable to the ladies, and that in this episode, Keats, whatever
his intentions, met the public's taste.

Romance fictions embody a period's dominant attitudes to sexuality. Here Keats speaks for his age's male-oriented fantasies in
which 'tender' women luxuriate in their subjection to men's passion. Lamia's dangerous shape-changing reflects an ambiguous
response to the conflicting and unstable roles imposed upon
women's sexuality by conventional expectations. *Lamia*, by
unintentionally exposing the subconscious patterns in a recurrent
early nineteenth-century 'love'-plot, forces its reader to a critique
of its inhumanity and limitations. Lamia, as the victim of a world
controlled by the overwhelming rationalism of the mature
Apollonius and the self-gratifying needs of the youthful Lycius'
sudden sexual awareness (I. 229), is truly to be pitied. But the
identification of Lamia with both Love and Poetry, and the
poem's varying tones, suggest an indirect relationship with
Keats's rejection of Love, Ambition, and the 'demon Poesy' in the

'Ode on Indolence'. Keats's own uncertainties intrude too openly for *Lamia* to attain any balance. The mutuality which characterises *The Eve of St Agnes*, or the 'unmisgiving' exploration of Isabella's madness, are abandoned for the sake of an illusory 'manly' objectivity.

Contradictory attitudes towards love, sexuality, and poetry lie behind the confusions of *Lamia*. They are openly expressed in four of the five poems associated with Keats's love for Fanny Brawne. 'The day is gone and all its sweets are gone!', 'I cry your mercy, pity, love – ay, love!', 'What can I do to drive away', and 'To Fanny' were probably written at the end of 1819 or even early in 1820. All four are unresolved in tone and subject, and marred by flaccid writing. They provide additional evidence to that given in the letters of Keats's loss of control over his conflicting emotions in the last months of 1819 and early 1820. Keats was ill, in love, but fearful of the future. His irrational jealousy of Fanny, which he had needed to control from the outset, was exacerbated by the fear that the twin commitments to poetry and love were mutually exclusive.

The poems are painful to read because they are private and desperately confused.[4] Only the 'Bright star' sonnet is in control of its emotions. Whether or not it belongs to the same late period as the other four lyrics is uncertain: the only hard evidence suggests a date at some time in 1819.[5] Like the spring odes, it begins by putting forward an apparently positive statement which is then partially withdrawn, and subsequently modified:

> Bright star! would I were steadfast as thou art –
>   Not in lone splendour hung aloft the night
> And watching, with eternal lids apart,
>   Like nature's patient, sleepless Eremite,
> The moving waters at their priestlike task
>   Of pure ablution round earth's human shores,
>   Or gazing on the new soft-fallen mask
> Of snow upon the mountains and the moors –
> No – yet still steadfast, still unchangeable,
>   Pillowed upon my fair love's ripening breast,
> To feel for ever its soft swell and fall,
>   Awake for ever in a sweet unrest,
> Still, still to hear her tender-taken breath,
> And so live ever – or else swoon to death.

The star's 'lone splendour' in watching over the natural world with an eremite's devotion, while the moving waters complete their purification of 'human shores', is an act of steadfast attentiveness.

Apart and alone, the star, 'with eternal lids apart', resembles the benign blankness of Moneta in *The Fall of Hyperion*, but the speaker's longing is not for identification with the star. Its inhuman steadfastness, eternal, world-embracing, and unsleeping, is transformed into a metaphor for the lover's wish for the eternal prolongation of the total absorption in the feel of his lover's living flesh. The poem's mingling of intimacy, wonder, and purity is dependent upon his awareness of her separateness. Despite the slippage in the final phrase ('or else swoon to death') into a lazily Keatsian commonplace, the sonnet's yearning for the star's 'steadfastness' and unchangeability, admits that human love cannot attain its calm certainty or eternity. The long moment may feel like a kind of sensual eternity, but, unlike the star's lonely splendour, the mutual pleasure of human lovers is only attainable or meaningful in a time-scale which includes change. 'My fair love's ripening breast' is a reminder of the fullness and richness of human satisfactions unavailable to the lonely disinterest of the star. Yet the superimposition of the star onto the two young lovers, while setting its all-seeing knowledge against the intense privacy of their intimacy, also suggests that their loss in one another's sensations has, for them at least, cosmic significance.

Love requires hubris ('We won't be like the others'), and love poetry speaks for that courage:

> For love, all love of other sights controules,
> And makes one little roome, an every where.
>
> (John Donne, 'The Good-morrow', lines 10–11)

Donne's masculinity differs from Keats's. While both insist upon the mutuality of sexual love, the strangeness of 'Bright star' is that while seeming to describe only the man's experience, it implies the feelings of both. Convention leads the reader to expect the opening image of the 'Bright star' to be used to describe the woman's qualities, but quite unexpectedly the sestet applies it to the man's yearnings. The waking passiveness is that of both man and woman, but, as is inevitable, only one side of the experience can be described. With the same fine balance of *The Eve of St Agnes*, the question of whether the emotions described precede or follow the lover's physical fulfilment is irrelevant: the essential feeling is true in either case. Unlike *Lamia*, 'Bright star' finds a humane resting point between the 'abstract adoration of the Deity' and the actuality of physical love, a balance which Keats feared he was incapable of attaining. As the closing line shows the attainment of such balance was a risky business: its fineness is the greater for that risk.

The difficulties of *Lamia* are caused by Keats's self-defensive aggression towards the reading public and by his reassessment of 'romance'. *The Fall of Hyperion* is untroubled by *Lamia's* self-divisions. It remained unpublished until 1857, and was regarded, by those who knew it, as inferior to the earlier *Hyperion*. The fragment discovers a mythic order of vision for Keats's secular humanism, paradoxically attaining a severe impersonality through intense subjectivity. *Hyperion* had tried to ensure epic objectivity by observing the fallen Titans and Apollo's apotheosis with detachment: the dream-vision of *The Fall of Hyperion*, precisely because it places the narrator's experience at the centre, provides a vehicle true to Keats's form of the Romantic experience. In *Hyperion* Keats transmutes Milton's Christian epic into a modern myth of the necessity of change and progress. *The Fall of Hyperion*, remodelling Dante's *Divine Comedy*, creates a purgatorial and redemptive pattern in which the modern poet is forced to question the limits and sufficiency of the imagination's claims to truth. Uncompromisingly harsh and modern, *The Fall* rejects Keats's earlier dreams of Beauty as luxuriant and self-indulgent, taking him back to the fundamental questions about the role of poetry posed, but not answered, at the very beginning of his poetic career in *Sleep and Poetry*.

Unlike *Hyperion*, the later poem is not about a revolution. Although Keats began to weave parts of the earlier epic into the last part of *The Fall*, they are irrelevant to the main thrust of the argument. These scenes are needed only to provide examples of pain and loss. The evolutionary optimism of *Hyperion* cannot be sustained since *The Fall of Hyperion* believes that suffering is necessary for the self-realisation of the poet and of mankind at large.

The imaginative centre of *The Fall of Hyperion* is the narrator's nightmare-like encounter with the goddess Moneta, and the realisation that the modern poet's burden is the pain of consciousness. Moneta is, as her name suggests, an admonitory figure. She is also addressed as Mnemosyne, and like her namesake in *Hyperion*, is the goddess of memory, mother of the muses, and foster-mother of Apollo. In *The Fall* Moneta does not participate in the action (the narrative fails to reach that point).

Instead, her role is that of Saturn's priestess and the narrator's guide and mentor. She combines in herself the roles of Dante's guides, Vergil and Beatrice. As the last Titan, honouring a long since deposed order of godhead, she preserves the memory of the Titans and their downfall, a memory which causes her anguish. She promises the narrator,

> 'My power, which to me is still a curse,
> Shall be to thee a wonder; for the scenes
> Still swooning vivid through my globed brain,
> With an electral changing misery,
> Thou shalt with those dull mortal eyes behold,
> Free from all pain, if wonder pain thee not.'   (I. 243–8)

But access to that 'high tragedy' (I. 277) must be earned. Keats's dream-vision describes a prolonged rite of passage, initiating the self-conscious poet into painful maturity.

The first stage is regressive. The dreamer wakes in a mysterious forest arbour (I. 19–38). Others have been there before him. As the bower's 'trellis vines' and 'floral censers' indicate, the partly consumed 'feast of summer fruits' symbolises the luxurious pleasures of Fancy, which is all that *Endymion* and the 'Ode to Psyche' now seem to represent. It is the 'Chamber of Maiden-Thought', the 'Life of Sensations' of the old Keatsian realm of Flora. The opening section, which ends involuntarily when the narrator drinks from a 'cool vessel', is a nostalgic but firm repudiation of Keats's previous work.[6]

The dreamer wakes in a vast 'sanctuary', so old that it seems to pre-date human history's 'superannuated realms' and even nature itself. This, Saturn's temple, is deliberately modelled on pagan antiquity.[7] Laid out in the form of a cross, it faces east, towards the sun's rising. Beneath 'An image, huge of feature as a cloud', is a raised altar tended by a figure burning incense (later revealed as Moneta), I. 65–105. There the dreamer must undergo a trial, a dying into life, as he struggles with prodigious effort to reach the altar's steps.

> Prodigious seemed the toil; the leaves were yet
> Burning – when suddenly a palsied chill
> Struck from the paved level up my limbs,
> And was ascending quick to put cold grasp
> Upon those streams that pulse beside the throat.
> I shrieked; and the sharp anguish of my shriek
> Stung my own ears – I strove hard to escape

> The numbness, strove to gain the lowest step.
> Slow, heavy, deadly was my pace: the cold
> Grew stifling, suffocating, at the heart;
> And when I clasped my hands I felt them not.
> One minute before death, my iced foot touched
> The lowest stair; and as it touched, life seemed
> To pour in at the toes: I mounted up   (I. 121–34)

The 'veiled shadow' explains:

> . . . 'Thou hast felt
> What 'tis to die and live again before
> Thy fated hour. That thou hadst power to do so
> Is thy own safety . . .
> None can usurp this height . . .
> But those to whom the miseries of the world
> Are misery, and will not let them rest.'   (I. 141–9)

In the ensuing exchange, Moneta makes an absolute division between 'dreamers' and 'poets' (I. 150–202).[8] The dreamer is 'less than' men who act in the world – 'What benefit canst thou do, or all thy tribe,/ To the great world?' The poem's opening question of whether the narrator is 'fanatic' or 'poet' is ominously reiterated:

> . . . 'Art thou not of the dreamer tribe?
> The poet and the dreamer are distinct,
> Diverse, sheer opposite, antipodes.
> The one pours out a balm upon the world,
> The other vexes it.'   (I. 198–202)

Moneta's tacit assent to the narrator's description of the true poet as 'A humanist, physician to all men' (I. 190) is a rejection of poetry which turns away from the 'great world'. Although Moneta never affirms that the narrator is a poet rather than a dreamer, in the act of rejecting his own past and confronting death, the dreamer transforms his poetic self. The metamorphosis is confirmed by the narrator's capacity to render the symbolic expressiveness of Moneta's unveiled face:

> But yet I had a terror of her robes,
> And chiefly of the veils, that from her brow
> Hung pale, and curtained her in mysteries
> That made my heart too small to hold its blood.
> This saw that Goddess, and with sacred hand
> Parted the veils. Then saw I a wan face,
> Not pined by human sorrows, but bright-blanched

By an immortal sickness which kills not;
It works a constant change, which happy death
Can put no end to; deathwards progressing
To no death was that visage; it had passed
The lily and the snow; and beyond these
I must not think now, though I saw that face –
But for her eyes I should have fled away.
They held me back, with a benignant light,
Soft-mitigated by divinest lids
Half closed, and visionless entire they seemed
Of all external things – they saw me not,
But in blank splendour beamed like the mild moon,
Who comforts those she sees not, who knows not
What eyes are upward cast.   (I. 251–71)

The reference to the moon is a reminder of how far *The Fall* is
from *Endymion*. Here the moon, 'mild' yet alien and 'blank',
benignant but visionless, is the moon we know. Moneta is not a
heavenly lover like Diana but an admonitory figure, closer to a
mother, with whom the would-be poet has to enter a relationship
which is wholly asexual. Moneta's inward vision contemplates the
inevitable suffering of the Titans. Her terrible knowledge of their
agony takes on a tragic impersonality which 'comforts those she
knows not', just as Keats's own 'contemplation of the inevitable
and endless suffering to which his more immediately personal
experience leads him has a like impersonal strength'.[9] Moneta's
otherness has a weird familiarity: in imagining her capacity to
contemplate suffering, without in any way losing the ability to feel
with its victims, Keats recognises and so creates his own spectral
self (Moneta's relation to Keats bears comparison with Rilke's
Angel).[10] It is a moment of profound poetic self-realisation.

As Marilyn Butler has pointed out, Keats's conception of *The
Fall* seems to be in some part a reply to Coleridge's 'Allegoric
Vision' in the second *Lay Sermon* (1817):

Coleridge's Dreamer encounters the false idol of the present day, whose real
name is Superstition, though he is worshipped by modern man as science or
materialism. He also meets (for she is much neglected) a statuesque goddess
who turns out to be Religion . . . In 'The Fall of Hyperion' the protagonist
also in a dream meets a goddess, impressive and forbidding, who does not
represent supernatural religion, as in Coleridge's version, but Coleridge's
false deity, humanism . . . He would appear to be invoking the Coleridge
location in order to refute Coleridge's conclusion.[11]

Keats's humanistic deity, Moneta, represents a stoic humanism
answering Coleridge's affirmation of Christianity.

Marilyn Butler sees the connection with Coleridge as one which firmly places *The Fall of Hyperion* in the 'classic contemporary literary controversy, between the poet as activist and physician, and the poet as visionary or dreamer'. The 'large self-worshippers' attacked in the curse on bad modern poets (I. 204–10) should include Coleridge as well as Wordsworth.[12]

However, the obscurities of *The Fall of Hyperion*'s allusions and allegory make precise identifications doubtful, and the evolutionary optimism of the earlier *Hyperion* is not shared, in the fragment as we have it, by Moneta. Keats's reason for abandoning *The Fall*, apart from its Miltonisms, seems to lie in the fracture between the earlier poem's optimism and the inwardness and doubt of the new one. *The Fall* was written during the intensely hard-working period spent away from London and its distractions, which lasted from late July until mid September, Keats's withdrawal into his own creativity during these weeks is caught in a letter to Reynolds of 24 August:

My own being which I know to be becomes of more consequence to me than the crowds of Shadows in the Shape of Man and women that inhabit a kingdom. The Soul is a world of itself and has enough to do in its own home . . . for the rest of Mankind they are as much a dream to me as Miltons Hierarchies [of angelic powers]. (Letters, ii. 146)

However, on 18 September, three days before announcing he had given up *The Fall of Hyperion* (*Letters*, ii. 167), Keats wrote his eloquent account of how 'All civi[liz]ed countries become gradually more enlighten'd and there should be a continual change for the better' (*Letters*, ii. 193–5). The immediate cause of this passage was that Keats, unexpectedly called away on a brief visit to London, found himself travelling about London on the very day, Monday, 13 September, that huge crowds welcomed the radical politician, Henry Hunt, to the city. (Hunt had presided at the reform meeting in Manchester on 16 August which led to the notorious Peterloo Massacre, the subject of Shelley's *Mask of Anarchy*.) Hunt's 'triumphal entry', observed by Keats, gave cause for renewed optimism in the possibility of political progress.[13] Rather than pointing to *The Fall*'s sub-text,[14] Keats's affirmation of political optimism in the letter of 18 September,[15] is a reaction against the inwardly tragic vision of Moneta.

Much closer in spirit to the narrator's encounter with Moneta is Keats's long account of the 'vale of Soul-making', written some months earlier on 21 April (*Letters*, ii. 101–3). There Keats sketches a 'system of Salvation' which, unlike Christianity, 'does not affront our reason and humanity'. The 'system' outlined is a long way from *Endymion*'s sensual humanism. Keats could not believe suffering essential to humanity's self-redemption. Christianity therefore affronts our humanity because, unable to believe that mankind is created to suffer, it ascribes the cause of evil to mankind's own Original Sin. It 'affronts our reason' because, having blamed the human condition upon man's innate sinfulness, Christianity then has to invent a divine interposition to bring about man's salvation.[16] Keats scornfully dismisses such a belief as misguided superstition:

The common cognomen of this world among the misguided and superstitious is 'a vale of tears' from which we are to be redeemed by a certain arbitrary interposition of God and taken to Heaven – What a little circumscribe[d] straightened notion! (*Letters*, ii. 101–2)

Keats proposes instead that the world is really a 'vale of Soul-making', in which each individual must work out his or her own salvation. Only if the individual heart feels and suffers the realities of the world can it transcend itself. The emphasis upon the individual is at the centre of Keats's formulation of his spiritual existentialism. Only by achieving 'identity' through openness to, and knowledge of, suffering can a 'soul' be created.

Keats explains the way in which the transformation takes place, first in abstract terms:

This is effected by three grand materials acting the one upon the other for a series of years – These three materials are the *Intelligence* – [that is] the *human heart* (as distinguished from intelligence or Mind) and the *World* or *Elemental space* suited for the proper action of *Mind and Heart* on each other for the purpose of forming the *Soul* or *Intelligence destined to possess the sense of Identity.* (*ibid.*, p. 102)

In his effort to explain what he 'can but dimly perceive', Keats gives a 'homely' example:

I will call the *world* a School instituted for the purpose of teaching little children to read – I will call the *human heart* the *horn Book* used in that School – and I will call the *Child able to read, the Soul* made from that *school* and its *hornbook.* Do you not see how necessary a World of Pains and troubles is to school an Intelligence and make it a soul? A Place where the heart must feel and suffer in a thousand diverse ways! Not merely is the Heart a Hornbook, It is the Minds Bible, it is the Minds experience, it is the teat from which the Mind or intelligence sucks its identity – As various as the Lives of Men are – so various become their souls, and thus does god make individual beings, Souls, Identical Souls of the sparks of his own essence. *(ibid., 102–3)*

Christianity's invention of heaven as a recompense for earthly suffering is, then, an insult to mankind's potential. Experience and suffering are essential for the self-education of the individual intelligence into a soul. Christianity is an affront to reason because it is only one of many versions of natural religion and, worse, a perverted version. Keats, influenced by Enlightenment thinking in general and by Voltaire in particular, argues that Christianity is derivative:

It is pretty generally suspected that the chr[i]stian scheme has been copied from the ancient persian and greek Philosophers. Why may they not have made this simple thing even more simple for common apprehension by introducing Mediators and Personages in the same manner as in the hethen mythologies abstractions are personified . . . For as one part of the human species must have their carved Jupiter; so another part must have the palpable and named Mediator [written 'Mediatior'] and saviour, their Christ their Oromanes and their Vishnu. *(ibid., p. 103)*

Keats's answer to Christianity is profoundly humanist, a humanism embodied in *The Fall of Hyperion*. Moneta is the narrator's 'mediator', and her demand that the 'dreamer' suffer begins the process by which the heart is educated.

That the vision's 'religious' dimension is to form the centre is hinted at by the obscure induction. The overall meaning is clear enough: Keats fears, and wishes the reader to know he fears, that the dream about to be related may be an illusion:

> Fanatics have their dreams, wherewith they weave
> A paradise for a sect: the savage too
> From forth the loftiest fashion of his sleep
> Guesses at Heaven; pity these have not
> Traced upon vellum or wild Indian leaf
> The shadows of melodious utterance.
> But bare of laurel they live, dream, and die;
> For Poesy alone can tell her dreams,
> With the fine spell of words alone can save
> Imagination from the sable charm
> And dumb enchantment . . .
> Whether the dream now purposed to rehearse
> Be Poet's or Fanatic's will be known
> When this warm scribe my hand is in the grave. (I. 1–18)

The primary reference in the first two lines is to religious

135

fanaticism,[17] but what at first seems to promise a demonstration of likeness ('Fanatics . . . the savage *too*'), turns out to be a distinction between opposites. The self-delusions of religion are dangerous ('paradise' perhaps hints at Christianity's superstitious belief in Heaven), whereas the loss of the savage's 'dreams' and 'loftiest' guesses is a matter for regret. It is quite clear from the general tenor of Keats's thinking about myth that the savage's 'melodious utterances' can only be their animist worship of nature. The whole passage suggests that poetry and religion have a common origin in the human imagination. The savage stands at the beginning of the slow quest through which true poetry and religion are created. Poetic and religious myths are, it is implied, historical phenomena, whose truth is relative.

The description of the religious paraphernalia abandoned in Saturn's temple is a pointer in the same direction.

> Upon the marble at my feet there lay
> Store of strange vessels and large draperies,
> Which needs had been of dyed asbestos wove,
> Or in that place the moth could not corrupt,
> So white the linen; so, in some, distinct
> Ran imageries from a sombre loom,
> All in a mingled heap confused there lay
> Robes, golden tongs, censer, and chafing-dish,
> Girdles, and chains, and holy jewelleries.   (I. 73–80)

The surreal time-scale places the whole scene within and without time. Although the temple seems older than time, these religious accoutrements are a mixture of classical, and Judaeo-Christian objects. (The last four lines seem to echo the directions given in *Exodus* to the Israelites for the furnishing of the tabernacle.)[18] There are other suggestions of Druidic and Egyptian religions. If Saturn's religion has been overthrown, so too contemporary world religions may be no more permanent.

Pastness and presentness have a disturbing relationship. The world of the Titans is so ancient that even the gods who displaced them, Apollo and the Olympians, have themselves been superseded. Yet the narrator twice invokes the 'faded far flown Apollo', as if he still might be prevailed on to function in the modern world ('far flown' might suggest he is still alive somewhere, however far off). The first invocation against bad contemporary poets goes unanswered, but the second is successful, securing the 'dreamer' insight to Moneta's mind:

>   . . . 'Shade of Memory!'
> Cried I, with act adorant at her feet,
> 'By all the gloom hung round thy fallen house,
> By this last Temple, by the golden age,
> By great Apollo, thy dear foster child,
> And by thyself, forlorn Divinity,
> The pale Omega of a withered race,
> Let me behold . . .'   (I. 282–9)

The Fall of Hyperion is an attempt, once more, to summon up a bygone mythology in modern times. Moneta does initiate the 'dreamer' into her vision, but in one important respect is mistaken. Despite her earlier promise that, as a human, the dreamer will experience 'wonder' but not pain (I. 247–8), the human visionary undergoes her pain in putting on her knowledge:

>   . . . Without stay or prop,
> But my own weak mortality, I bore
> The load of this eternal quietude,
> The unchanging gloom, and the three fixed shapes
> Ponderous upon my senses a whole moon.
> For by my burning brain I measured sure
> Her silver seasons shedded on the night,
> And every day by day methought I grew
> More gaunt and ghostly. Oftentimes I prayed
> Intense, that Death would take me from the vale
> And all its burthens. Gasping with despair
> Of change, hour after hour I cursed myself   (I. 388–99)

The dreamer has become Moneta. Like her, he suffers from an immortal sickness which kills not. Negative capability's empathic vision, shared by both, finds knowledge only through suffering. Death, pain, and loss cannot be explained away, but *The Fall of Hyperion*'s fiction offers the consolation of knowledge through a contemplation of their necessity. *Endymion*'s Religion of Beauty and Joy has matured into a tragic 'religion' of the heart.

The alienated poet of *The Fall*, bearing the cost of consciousness, and employing the impersonality of mask, persona, or anti-self to objectify subjective understanding into a dialectic with reality or history, is central to post-Romantic poetry. Yet Keats's inability to complete *The Fall* suggests that he may have feared that the creation of his spectral self in Moneta was ultimately involved in the circularity of a disguised solipsism. The fragment might be read as not only prefiguring the impersonality of the artist which fascinated Symbolist poets from Mallarmé to Yeats, but as end-stopping that tradition, doubting its access to common experience.

'To Autumn' gives a naturalistic answer to the questions posed about the inevitability of change and death by the spring odes and *The Fall of Hyperion*. Keats described the poem's starting point in a letter of 21 September 1819:

> How beautiful the season is now – How fine the air. A temperate sharpness about it. Really, without joking, chaste weather – Dian skies – I never lik'd stubble fields so much as now – Aye better than the chilly green of the spring. Somehow a stubble plain looks warm – in the same way that some pictures look warm – this struck me so much in my sunday's walk that I composed upon it. (*Letters*, ii. 167)

Despite the letter's reference to 'Dian', direct classical references are strikingly absent from the ode. However, the restrained personifications create a figure in the landscape, an androgynous tutelary spirit who mingles natural process and human activity.[19] For Keats here, as elsewhere in his poetry, autumn is the time of fulfilment, plenitude, and harvest.[20] The whole poem is structured in answer to the question posed at the beginning of the third stanza, 'Where are the songs of spring? Ay, where are they?' This powerful threat to the celebration of autumn calls up the alternative image of autumn as a melancholy precursor of winter and death. The ode's reply is silently argued through its images and its plot. The annual cycle of the seasons, the movement from rebirth to death, is as natural to man as it is to nature. Without autumn's movement into winter there could be no spring. Human and natural life are intrinsically tied to the pattern of change and renewal. Autumn's beauty is particular to itself, dependent upon the fact that it is neither winter, spring, nor summer. Hence, 'thou hast thy music too'.

The shaping of the ode's plot follows the movement from preharvest ripeness in the first stanza, to the satiated fullness of harvest in the second, and concludes in the poignant emptiness following the completion of harvest and immediately preceding winter. Each stanza is poised at a turning point in one of the phases of autumn, and each shows nature in a different relationship to mankind. In the first stanza, autumn, 'Season of mists and mellow fruitfulness', conspires with the 'maturing sun' to fill 'all fruit with ripeness to the core'. Their conspiracy is that of 'Close bosom-friends' – the sun is explicitly characterised as male, but 'bosom-friends' holds off the suggestion that autumn should be seen as female: their mysterious conspiracy to create the bursting fullness of the fruit and flowers, though of benefit to mankind, is not to be understood by a direct analogy to human fertility. Throughout the first stanza mankind is just off-stage. The 'thatch eves', 'mossed cottage-trees', gourds, and bees belong to the gardens of England's cottagers, and the dominance of tactile imagery indicates that the focus is on nature's strange power to 'plump' and 'swell' the vegetable world rather than upon the part played by man's cultivation (that is assumed to have happened earlier).

The second stanza presents autumn as four figures completing harvest tasks. They are less English farm-workers than symbols of the beneficent cooperation between natural and human activity which leads to harvest. The opening lines make pretence that every reader has or can see these figures, a manoeuvre which presses us to accede to, indeed, to create for ourselves, the poem's pastoral idyll:

> Who hath not seen thee oft amid thy store?
>   Sometimes whoever seeks abroad may find
> Thee sitting careless on a granary floor,
>   Thy hair soft-lifted by the winnowing wind;
> Or on a half-reaped furrow sound asleep,
>   Drowsed with the fume of poppies, while thy hook
> Spares the next swath and all its twined flowers:
>   And sometimes like a gleaner though dost keep
> Steady thy laden head across a brook;
>   Or by a cider-press, with patient look,
> Thou watchest the last oozings hours by hours.

As portrayed here, Autumn hovers between real workers and allegorical manifestations, and between male and female. Although men and women worked together in the fields, reaping was the work of men or boys, gleaning the work of women and children. The depiction of the 'reaper' with a 'hook' rather than a scythe links him with eighteenth-century portrayals of Autumn as a man with a sickle,[21] but the poppies, while real enough in a cornfield, suggest the presence of Ceres, the Roman goddess of corn and harvests. Lemprière says, 'Ceres was represented with a garland of ears of corn on her head, holding in one hand a lighted torch, and in the other a poppy, which was sacred to her.' The reaper, 'sound asleep', is not simply an English labourer exhausted by toil: the poppies arrest the reaper in mid action in reproach for the necessary destruction of the beauty of 'the next swath and all its twined flowers'. Autumn's generosity in meeting humanity's needs involves giving of itself, so much so, it is hinted, that Autumn does the work for mankind. That is why, with the exception of the gleaner, the figures are inactive or asleep. The wind, having winnowed the grain, now idly lifts the sleeper's hair in the granary, the poppies overcome the reaper, and the cider-press's 'last oozings hours by hours' seem more accomplished by the fruits themselves than by any human intervention. Assenting to this pastoral vision means perceiving that the hard human labour of harvesting is dependent upon nature's benevolence for its success.

The final stanza turns away from man to autumn's music. Contained between the 'barred clouds' of 'the soft-dying day' and the earth of the 'stubble-plain' are the mingled sounds of non-human life. Ranging from the 'wailful choir of gnats' to the bleatings of the 'full-grown lambs', the music includes the sounds of natural life which simply continues, unaware of man, and those of animals cultivated by man. The robin, whistling from a 'garden-croft', is somewhere between wild and tame, while the swallow, wild yet often choosing to nest in buildings to which it returns annually, suggests that a common pattern of loss and return governs both human and non-human life. Like the 'full-grown lambs', the swallow is a reminder of the inevitable return of spring and renewal. With an effortless tact, arising from a sharp sense of the separateness of human and non-human life, 'To Autumn' intimates how the two share in one another's existence, and stresses mankind's dependence upon and final oneness with the natural world.[22] 'To Autumn' is, of course, a fiction, and as pastoral celebrates an ideal relation between man and nature. It is a consolation and an affirmation of a necessary balance. It is not merely a fiction about a fiction, nor is it a reactionary escape from reality.[23] Fictions, as well as telling untruths, tell truths.

Conclusion

Keats's 'sensual humanism',[1] with its commitment to an aesthetic axis, has Continental parallels but is unique in English Romantic poetry. Although the reviews of the *Lamia* volume were generally favourable, his poetry found few early readers (Taylor had sold less than 500 copies after two years and was still advertising the first edition in 1828[2]). However, Keats's example was important for nineteenth-century poetry. Its influence on the early Tennyson, the Pre-Raphaelites, Hopkins and on Victorian Aestheticism opens up a line of development which owes nothing to Wordsworth, Shelley, or Byron. The Victorian sentimentalisation of Keats misses, however, the essentially honest and questioning nature of his work. Keats never believed in 'Art for Art's sake', even though *Endymion*'s opening proposition, 'A thing of beauty is a joy for ever', risks leading him in that direction. The successful mature poetry, sceptical and explorative, struggles to face the problem of time, loss, and suffering while maintaining its belief in the sustaining powers of the human imagination.

The successes in Keats's body of poetry were, however, won at a price. There is always a gap between the language of poetry and the language of prose and speech. The gap was a matter of acute anxiety for the Romantics (Keats's stated reason for abandoning *The Fall of Hyperion* was that its diction was too Miltonic[3]). Keats's conscious archaism, distinctive vocabulary, and his constant allusions to other literatures, poets, or mythologies, all declare the 'literariness' of his poetry. For him, poetry's language was necessarily different from that of common speech. The 'dreams of art', the attempt to limn out imaginative 'realms', require, Keats believed, their own language.

Even a cursory comparison of Keats's letters with his poetry raises the question of whether too much of life and vitality is sacrificed to the constriction of style and subject matter imposed by the willed pursuit of 'Beauty' and the straining after 'Truth'. There is nothing in the poems to compare with the partly admiring, partly exasperated, partly affectionate account of Keats's conversation with Coleridge:

I met Mr Green our Demonstrator at Guy's in conversation with Coleridge – I joined them, after enquiring by a look whether it would be agreeable – I walked with him a[t] his alderman-after dinner pace for near two Miles I suppose[.] In those two Miles he broached a thousand things – let me see if I can give you a list – Nightingales, Poetry – on Poetical sensation – Metaphysics – Different genera and species of Dreams – Nightmare – a dream accompanied by a sense of touch – single and double touch – A dream related – First and second consciousness – the difference explained between will and Volition – so m[a]ny metaphysicians from a want of smoking the second consciousness – Monsters – the Kraken – Mermaids – southey believes in them – southeys belief too much diluted – A Ghost story – Good morning – I heard his voice as he came towards me – I heard it as he moved away – I had heard it all the interval – if it may be called so. He was civil enough to ask me to call on him at Highgate.

(*Letters*, ii. 88–9)

Nor can the poetry find a way to express Keats's moral outrage at the social injustice and exploitation which he saw in Ireland:

On our return from Bellfast we met a Sedan [written 'Sadan'] – the Duchess of Dunghill – It is no laughing matter tho – Imagine the worst dog kennel you ever saw placed upon two poles from a mouldy fencing – In such a wretched thing sat a squalid old Woman squat like an ape half starved from a scarcity of Buiscuit in its passage from Madagascar to the cape, – with a pipe in her mouth and looking out with a round-eyed skinny lidded, inanity – with a sort of horizontal idiotic movement of her head – squab and lean she sat and puff'd out the smoke while two ragged tattered Girls carried her along – What a thing would be a history of her Life and sensations. (*Letters*, i. 321–2)

Although Keats disliked 'description', his long account of Fingal's Cave is deftly precise, evocative and witty (*Letters*, i. 348–9), and directly realised. The same sense of physical actuality is caught in Keats's excited reaction on seeing the waterfalls and mountains of the Lake District.

First we stood a little below the head [of the waterfall] about half way down the first fall, buried deep in trees, and saw it streaming down two more descents to the depth of near fifty feet – then we went out on a jut of rock nearly level with the second fall-head, where the first fall was above us, and the third below our feet still – at the same time we saw that the water was divided by a sort of cataract island on whose other side burst out a glorious stream – then the thunder and the freshness. At the same time the different falls have as different characters; the first darting down the slate-rock like an arrow; the second spreading out like a fan –

the third dashed into a mist – and the one on the other side of the rock a sort of mixture of all these. We afterwards moved away a space, and saw nearly the whole more mild, streaming silverly through the trees. What astonishes me more than any thing is the tone, the coloring, the slate, the stone, the moss, the rock-weed; or, if I may so say, the intellect, the countenance of such places. The space, the magnitude of mountains and waterfalls are well imagined before one sees them; but this countenance or intellectual tone must surpass every imagination and defy any remembrance. I shall learn poetry here and shall henceforth write more than ever, for the abstract endeavor of being able to add a mite to that mass of beauty which is harvested from these grand materials, by the finest spirits, and put into etherial existence for the relish of one's fellows.

(Letters, i. 300–1)

Poetry's need to 'etherialise' the particularity and lively awe of this account into an abstracted 'relish' for humanity works against the kind of vivid life of the letter's unaffected prose.

The letters, whose enthusiasm and idealism is always brought to earth by Keats's ironic self-awareness, have a firm sense of the difference between fancy and actuality. Writing to Mrs James Wylie from Scotland, he says,

But I must leave joking & seriously aver, that I have been *werry* romantic indeed, among these Mountains & Lakes. I have got wet through day after day, eaten oat cake, & drank whiskey, walked up to my knees in Bog, got a sore throat, gone to see Icolmkill & Staffa, met with wholesome food, just here & there as it happened; went up Ben Nevis, & N.B. came down again; Sometimes when I am rather tired, I lean rather languishingly on a Rock, & long for some famous Beauty to get down from her Palfrey in passing; approach me with – her saddle bags – & give me – a dozen or two capital roast beef sandwiches. *(Letters,* i. 359–60)

The attempt to play between the attractions of romance and the knowledge of life in *The Eve of St Agnes* and *Lamia* threatens the very fabric of the poetry. Its truthfulness, like that of all poetry, depends upon exclusion in order to explore the particular.

There is a case for arguing that Keats's letters are finer than his poetry. We can certainly see from them that little of his remarkable ear for the spoken language, or his lively interest in slang and colloquialisms, appears in the serious poetry. So, too, the volatility and mobility of Keats's mind and temperament are portrayed with a directness impossible in the poems.

The contrast between the poems and the letters points to a central feature of Romantic literature, its wish to break down the traditional categorisation of experience by genre. The traditional elevation of poetry over prose, a superiority which Keats, Shelley, and Wordsworth believed in, was in fact powerfully, if implicitly, challenged by major currents in the period. Much of Romanticism is characterised by a drive towards realism, and by the denial of the conventional organisation of experience into the hierarchical genre divisions of earlier literature. The traditional forms denied the multiplicity of individual human experience. Heterogeneity, process, the breaking down of divisions, and the registration of the variety and importance of the individual's perception of self and the surrounding world, characterise one side of Romanticism. Equally, the need to change the *status quo*, a drive towards realism and activism, characterise another. For all these prose was the natural form of expression. Quite apart from the importance of the novels of Scott, Jane Austen, Mary Shelley, and Maria Edgeworth, the richness and variety of the period's achievement in forms like the essay, autobiographical or confessional works, and journalism deny the tidy and simple divisions implied by inherited genres. Hazlitt, Lamb, and De Quincey sit oddly in the Romantic pantheon, yet demand attention. Romantic poetry finds it hard to come to terms with prosaic day-to-day living, and finds it even more difficult to express. Consequently, non-fictional prose, perceived as less self-conscious than poetry, was hospitable to the contradictory impulses within Romanticism, and ranges from self-explorations in diary, letters or autobiography to social and political analysis and exhortation in the essay or pamphlet.

These 'sub-literary' forms are major vehicles for the expression of the Romantic imagination, and Keats's letters, like those of the other great Romantic letter writers, should be considered alongside the other prose writings of the period. Keats remarked, with some obscurity, 'Shakspeare led a life of Allegory; his works are the comments on it' (*Letters*, ii. 67).[4] This is impossible to apply to the historical Shakespeare, but does offer a description of Keats's own correspondence. Among other things, the letters provide an account of the poet's development, and a portrait of the artist as a young man. They are part of the process by which Keats became a poet and at the same time a manifestation of the self-creating imagination. Editors and commentators read the letters as notes on the poems because that is their job. It is quite possible to read the letters in their own right as the autobiography of Keats's imaginative quest, as his *Prelude*, but a *Prelude* unmediated by memory, and one which admits to the contradictions and tensions between Beauty and Knowledge.

The stylistic distance between Keats's letters and the poems he published during his lifetime is an extreme example of Romantic poetry's difficulty in admitting contemporary life and speech into its fictions. Yet some of the personal and playful verse Keats wrote for himself or to others show a wider range of style than appears in his formal poetry. The delightfully self-mocking account he wrote to his young sister Fanny during his Northern walking tour is proof of a talent for light verse:

> There was a naughty boy,
> A naughty boy was he,
> He would not stop at home
> He could not quiet be –
> He took
> In his knapsack
> A book
> Full of vowels
> And a shirt
> With some towels –
> A slight cap
> For night-cap –
> A hair brush,
> Comb ditto,
> New stockings,
> For old ones
> Would split O!
> This knapsack
> Tight at's back
> He rivetted close
> And follow'd his nose
> To the North,
> To the North,
> And follow'd his nose
> To the North.   (lines 1–25)

There is also the playful address 'To Mrs Reynolds's Cat' ('Cat! who hast past thy grand climacteric,/ How many mice and rats hast in thy days/ Destroyed? . . .'), charming and slight, but self-assured.

But light poetry did not offer Keats a way of extending his serious poetic idiom. Faced with the same problem, other second generation Romantic poets were able to find ways to include more of contemporary life and language. Shelley's verse epistles, like that to Maria Gisborne, use the informality of the letter to follow the flow of his intelligence, creating a highly personal poetry,

colloquial, immediate, relaxed, and yet intense. The nearest
Keats comes to doing so is in the verse letter to Reynolds (the
epistles published in *Poems* (1817) are mere occasions for 'poetry').
Its opening is strikingly direct and disconcerting:

> Dear Reynolds, as last night I lay in bed,
> There came before my eyes that wonted thread
> Of shapes, and shadows, and remembrances,
> That every other minute vex and please:
> Things all disjointed come from North and South –
> Two witch's eyes above cherub's mouth,
> Voltaire with casque and shield and habergeon,
> And Alexander with his nightcap on,
> Old Socrates a-tying his cravat,
> And Hazlitt playing with Miss Edgeworth's cat,
> And Junius Brutus, pretty well so so,
> Making the best of's way towards Soho.   (lines 1–12)

Revealing and interesting as the epistle is, it cannot survive the
realisation of nature's 'fierce destruction' (line 102). As a poem it
is broken-backed, defeated by its material. Nor does Keats show
any signs of developing a dramatised modern conversation poem
like Shelley's *Julian and Maddalo*. Yet it is symptomatic of the power
of contemporary notions of poetic style that Shelley himself did not
fully recognise the potential of these conversational and confessional
forms to release the modern poet from the restrictions of a 'high'
style. The epistle to Maria Gisborne was not intended for publication, and he was uneasy about *Julian and Maddalo*. Shelley wanted
the poem, now regarded as a major work, published anonymously
and separately from his lyric drama, *Prometheus Unbound*. He
explained, 'It is an attempt in a different style, in which I am not
yet sure of myself, a *sermo pedestris* [prosaic] way of treating human
nature quite opposed to the idealism of that drama.'[5] The
'idealisms' of poetry excluded the prose of contemporary life.

The poetic form which did allow the portrayal of everyday life
and the use of colloquial speech was, as Byron demonstrated,
satire or serio-comic poetry. Both forms make full use of irony and
deploy a variety of tones, precisely the effects Keats was pursuing
in *Lamia*. Keats's few efforts in this direction are unconvincing.
His satire on modern lovers, apparently written extemporarily in
a letter to the George Keatses (*Letters*, ii. 188), quickly peters out,
but has a certain effectiveness:

> Pensive they sit, and roll their languid eyes,
> Nibble their toasts and cool their tea with sighs;

Or else forget the purpose of the night,
Forget their tea, forget their appetite.
See, with crossed arms they sit – Ah! hapless crew,
The fire is going out and no one rings
For coals, and therefore no coals Betty brings.
A fly is in the milk-pot – must he die
Circled by a Humane Society?
No, no; there, Mr. Werter takes his spoon,
Inverts it, dips the handle, and lo! soon
The little struggler, saved from perils dark,
Across the teaboard draws a long wet mark.   (lines 1–13)

But Keats is only idling away time: the fragment has no direction. His one serious effort to write a serio-comic poem, the unfinished 'The Cap and Bells: or, The Jealousies', is obscure and rambling. Probably intended as a mixture of satire on contemporary literature and politics,[6] the tale rises above fanciful obscurity at a few points. The comic curse directed at London's hackney coachmen and their equipages takes the city's most ubiquitous form of travel as its target:

Polluted Jarvey! Ah, thou filthy hack!
Whose springs of life are all dried up and dead,
Whose linsey-woolsey lining hangs all slack,
Whose rug is straw, whose wholeness is a crack;
And evermore thy steps go clatter-clitter;
Whose glass once up can never be got back,
Who prov'st, with jolting arguments and bitter,
That 'tis of modern use to travel in a litter.   (lines 227–34)

Similarly, an earlier comic fragment, is a lively evocation of contemporary London:

Sir, Convent Garden is a monstrous beast;
From morning, four o'clock, to twelve at noon,
It swallows cabbages with a spoon,
And then, from twelve till two, this Eden made is
A promenade for cooks and ancient ladies;
And then for supper, 'stead of soups and poaches,
It swallows chairmen, damns, and hackney coaches.
('Fragment of the "Castle-Builder"', lines 9–15)

These passages have vitality of a kind. Leigh Hunt's use of Keats's three stanzas on the hackney coach ('The Cap and Bells', lines 217–57) in his essay on 'Coaches' in the *Indicator* of 23 August 1820, is interesting. Their publication (anonymously) in Hunt's essay suggests that Keats had the capacity to write the fanciful prose pieces on contemporary life written by Hunt himself, Charles Lamb, and other periodical writers.

But Keats's dedication to a high-minded view of Poetry and Fame meant that any talent for whimsical or light verse, or for satire, went undeveloped. The true Keats is, in the end, the 'un-misgiving' Keats, pursuing Beauty and Truth, but too honest to accept their proffered haven at face value. Keats's commonsense questioning of the claims of the imagination is that of the ordinary reader. It matters that Keats's powerful claims for the imagination's truth have to be set unequivocally against the demands of actuality.

> Fled is that music – Do I wake or sleep?

The answer lies with the reader and the reader's experience of the poem, but the 'Ode to a Nightingale', like Keats's poetry as a whole, affirms the consolations art affords humanity even while warning of its limits. The maturity of Keats's poetry shares, with the letters, a firm sense of what words can and cannot do:

Writing has this disadvan[ta]ge of speaking. one cannot write a wink, or a nod, or a grin, or a purse of the Lips, or a *smile* – *O law!* One can[not] put ones finger to one's nose, or yerk ye in the ribs, or lay hold of your button in writing . . .   (*Letters*, ii. 205)

Appendix: The poems to Fanny Brawne

Paul de Man believes that *Lamia* and *The Fall of Hyperion* are 'works of transition toward a new phase that is fully revealed only in the last poems [the lyrics to Fanny] Keats wrote' (*The Selected Poetry of Keats* (New York, 1963, etc.), p. xxvii). Since de Man's edition is cheap and widely available, it is an important matter that de Man's treatment of these poems is acutely misleading.

With the exception of the 'Bright star' sonnet, these poems cannot be understood outside their place in Keats's biography. They were written late in 1819 or in 1820, and relate to the painfully confused letters which Keats wrote to Fanny Brawne early in 1820 after his first haemorrhage.[1] In this context, the meaning of the poems is distressingly obvious. Keats's earlier fear that love was incompatible with a career as a poet becomes a strident obsession. The other subject is the ugly anxiety produced by irrational jealousy. The callow ode 'To Fanny' contains all the elements (significantly, de Man truncates this embarrassing poem). Keats begins by asking 'Physician Nature' to 'ease my heart of verse' (lines 1–2), so that he can begin his dream of Fanny (lines 7–8). A single stanza describes his vassalage to her beauty: the remaining five are given over to a desperate plea that Fanny spare him from 'torturing jealousy' (line 48). The reference to the 'wintry air' (line 8), and the fact that Fanny appears to be free to go to dances (lines 25–7), link it to the period early in 1820 when the sick Keats, secretly engaged to Fanny, was kept to his room, while living next door to her. He was able to see Fanny only briefly or through the window. His jealousy, there from the beginning of their relationship, became contorted into a self-lacerating anxiety. Keats's fear is that the 'Voluptuous visions' of music and the 'dance's dangerous wreath' (lines 25–7) will lead Fanny to flirt with her admirers, for women are, by nature, fickle:

> . . . confess – 'tis nothing new –
> Must not a woman be
> A feather on the sea,
> Swayed to and fro by every wind and tide?
> Of as uncertain speed
> As blow-ball from the mead?   (lines 35–40)

The final stanza (simply omitted by de Man) employs sacramental imagery, as coy as it is coarse, to hide a disfiguring need for, and disbelief in the possibility of, Fanny's utter purity of mind and body:

> Let none profane my Holy See of Love,
>> Or with a rude hand break
>> The sacramental cake;
> Let none else touch the just new-budded flower;
>> If not – may my eyes close,
>> Love! on their last repose.

As most earlier critics have seen, this is the bullying fearfulness of an ill man who had lost balance.

The sonnet, 'I cry your mercy, pity, love – ay, love!', deals with the same themes. The poem invokes 'guileless love . . . without a blot!', and asks 'O! let me have thee whole, – all, all, be mine!' (lines 1–5). A swift move to the Endymionese attractions of 'That warm, white, lucent, million-pleasured breast', soon turns back to the earlier demand. 'Withhold no atom's atom or I die' (lines 6–10). The fear is clear enough: women's love cannot be without blot. Simultaneously, Keats fears that love will 'enthrall' his poetic ambitions:

> Or living on perhaps, your wretched thrall,
>> Forget, in the mist of idle misery,
> Life's purposes – the palate of my mind
> Losing its gust, and my ambition blind!

'The day is gone, and all its sweets are gone!' begins by regressing to early Keats ('Sweet voice, sweet lips, soft hand, and softer breast'), moves momentarily to real intensity –

> When the dusk holiday – or holinight –
> Of fragrant-curtained love begins to weave
> The woof of darkness, thick, for hid delight
>
> (lines 10–12)

– before concluding limply with the hope that he will be allowed to sleep that night. 'What can I do to drive away' is a discordant jarring of emotions and thoughts, and Keats has only half his mind on Fanny. On the one hand, Keats wants 'to kill' love and 'be free' to write poetry, to regain his poetic wings,

> . . . and so mount once more
> Above, above
> The reach of fluttering Love,
> And make him cower lowly while I soar.   (lines 20–23)

But the effusion closes with Keats imagining holding Fanny in his arms – 'Enough! Enough! it is enough for me/ To dream of thee!' The poem makes quite clear that it wasn't enough. Keats wanted Fanny, he wanted to write poetry, and he wanted to be relieved of the worry he felt about his brother in America. The only powerful lines in the poem describe the New World as a wasteland – vast, new, and with no mythology:

> . . . that most hateful land,
> Dungeoner of my friends, that wicked strand
> Where they were wrecked and live a wrecked life;
> That monstrous region, whose dull rivers pour
> Ever from their sordid urns into the shore,
> Unowned of any weedy-haired gods;
> Whose winds, all zephyrless, hold scourging rods,
> Iced in the great lakes, to afflict mankind;
> Whose rank-grown forests, frosted, black, and blind,
> Would fright a Dryad; whose harsh-herbaged meads
> Make lean and lank the starved ox while he feeds;
> There flowers have no scent, birds no sweet song,
> And great unerring Nature once seems wrong.
>
> (lines 31–43)

The poem's unprepared jump to this topic assumes that Fanny knows what Keats is talking about. An outsider has no clue that the 'monstrous region' is America, or that the 'friends' are his brother and his family.

In all four late poems, the relation between poetry and life is threateningly confused – in one letter to Fanny Keats quotes from 'Isabella' to express his feelings (*Letters*, ii. 256). The fact that Fanny Brawne kept copies of these poems, which must have caused her pain, shows a generous understanding of the extremities to which Keats was driven by illness and his anxieties about the future. It is a generosity posterity ought to respect.

There is one final poem, sometimes associated with Fanny Brawne, sometimes thought to be a scrap for a possible drama, written late in 1819. Given the feelings expressed it can hardly have been addressed to Fanny, and seems, unlike the personal lyrics addressed to Fanny, to be a purely private poem:

> This living hand, now warm and capable
> Of earnest grasping, would, if it were cold
> And in the icy silence of the tomb,
> So haunt thy days and chill thy dreaming nights
> That thou would wish thine own heart dry of blood

So in my veins red life might stream again,
And thou be conscience-calmed – see here it is –
I hold it towards you.

The fact that Keats did become a major poet gives these lines an unanswerable poignancy. It is almost an epigraph to the poetry, demonstrating poetry's effort to 'grasp' the reader from beyond the grave, an attempt of no help to the dying Keats. Poetry is turned, ineffectually, against the living.

Notes

1. An early nineteenth-century poet

1 Amy Clampitt, 'Margate', 'Voyages: A Homage to John Keats', in *What the Light was Like* (New York, 1985), p. 47.

2 *John Keats: The Complete Poems*, ed. John Barnard (Harmondsworth, 2nd edn, 1976). All quotations are from this text. Reference is also made to *The Poems of John Keats*, ed. Jack Stillinger (Cambridge, Mass., 1978). The quotations from Lemprière's *Bibliotheca Classica* . . . (2nd edn, 1792) are reprinted in Barnard, ed., *John Keats*, pp. 697–719.

3 *The Letters of John Keats*, ed. Hyder E. Rollins (Cambridge, Mass., 1958), i. 141. All subsequent references are to this edition.

4 W. J. Bate, *John Keats* (Cambridge, Mass., 1963; rptd 1967), pp. 14–15.

5 August 1818. Cited from the extracts printed in *The Young Romantics and Critical Opinion 1807–1824*, ed. Theodore Redpath (1973), p. 472.

6 *The British Critic*, June 1818, *ibid.*, p. 68.

7 *Ibid.*, pp. 68, 471.

8 For *The Quarterly*'s circulation see Richard D. Altick, *The English Common Reader* (Chicago, 1957; rptd 1963), p. 392. On *The Examiner* see John O. Hayden, *The Romantic Reviewers 1802–1824* (Chicago, 1969), pp. 66–7: its circulation probably reached a peak of 7,000 to 8,000 in 1812, but had declined to 3,200 by 1819.

9 *Recollections of Writers* (1878), ed. Robert Gittings (Fontwell, Sussex, 1969), p. 124. For the influence of Gilbert Burnet's *The History of My Own Times* (1723–34), see Robert M. Ryan, *Keats: The Religious Sense* (Princeton, 1976), pp. 40–43.

10 *Letters*, i, 187n. See Redpath, ed., *Young Romantics*, pp. 510–11, for a quotation from Scott's review.

11 Richard Holmes, *Shelley the Pursuit* (1974; 1976), pp. 148–50.

12 'Lines Written on 29 May, The Anniversary of the Restoration of Charles the 2nd'.

13 *Revaluation: Tradition and Development in English Poetry* (1936), p. 259.

14 *Letters*, i. 86.

15 Quoted by Tim Chilcott, *A Publisher and his Circle: The Life and Works of John Taylor, Keats's Publisher* (1972), p. 25. The details here and in the following paragraphs are taken from Chilcott's book (*passim*).

16 See Chilcott, *A Publisher*, pp. 131–2.

17 For the information on Bloomfield, see Chilcott, *A Publisher*, p. 10.

The other source for the figures in this paragraph is Altick, *English Common Reader*, pp. 262–3, 325, 381.

[18] 'Preface to the *Lyrical Ballads*', *William Wordsworth: The Poems*, ed. John O. Hayden (Harmondsworth, 1977), i. 872–3.

[19] *The Spirit of the Age*, *The Complete Works*, ed. P. P. Howe (1930–34), xi. 38.

[20] *Ibid.*, xi. 124.

[21] *The Life of Napoleon*, *The Complete Works*, ed. P. P. Howe (1930–34), xiii. 38. For Keats's agreement, see the fragment, 'In after-time, a sage of mickle lore', probably written in July 1820. The stanza rewrites Spenser's anti-democratic allegory in *The Faerie Queeene*, V.ii. 29–54. Spenser's 'mighty Gyant', who demands equality for all, is opposed by Artegall (Justice, and representative of the English crown in Ireland) and overthrown by Talus (the executive arm of the government). Keats's 'Giant' of the future, aided by the wisdom of 'Typographus' (the modern press), overcomes his two oppressors.

[22] *Spirit of the Age*, ed. Howe, p. 139.

[23] Chilcott, *A Publisher*, p. 41.

2. 'Energy and Voluptuousness': *Poems* (1817)

[1] Charles and Mary Cowden Clarke, *Recollections of Writers* (1878), ed. Robert Gittings (Fontwell, Sussex, 1969), p. 126.

[2] *The Faerie Queene*, II. xii. 23.

[3] *Keats: The Critical Heritage*, ed. G. M. Matthews (1971), pp. 368–9.

[4] Cited in *The Young Romantics and Critical Opinion, 1807–1834*, ed. Theodore Redpath, p. 422n.

[5] See *John Keats: The Complete Poems*, ed. John Barnard (Harmondsworth, 2nd edn, 1976), p. 655.

[6] The point is Kenneth Muir's, 'The Meaning of *Hyperion*', *John Keats: A Reassessment*, ed. Muir (Liverpool, 1958), p. 116.

[7] See John Bayley's important essays on Keats in *The Uses of Division: Unity and Disharmony in Literature* (1976), pp. 107–56.

[8] Unsigned review in *The Indicator*, 2, 9 August 1820. Rptd in *Young Romantics*, ed. Redpath, p. 499.

[9] *The Golden Treasury* (1861), p. 320.

[10] *Keats's Metaphors for the Poetic Imagination* (Durham, N.C., 1967), pp. 164, 167 *passim*.

[11] Unsigned review in *The Champion*, 9 March 1817. Rptd *Young Romantics*, ed. Redpath, p. 451.

[12] The title page has the epigraph, 'What more felicity can fall to creature,/ Than to enjoy delight with liberty' (Spenser, *Muiopotmos*, lines 209–10).The half title to the Epistles has 'Among the rest a skill/ His few yeares could, began to fit his quill' (William Browne,

Britannia's Pastorals, II. iii. 748–50). Stillinger, following Stuart Sperry, thinks the vignette head represents Spenser not Shakespeare as is usually thought (*The Poems of John Keats*, ed. Jack Stillinger, Cambridge, Mass., 1978, p. 736).

[13] Stuart M. Sperry, 'Richard Woodhouse's Interleaved and Annotated Copy of Keats's *Poems* (1817)', *Literary Monographs* I, ed. E. Rothstein and T. K. Dunseath (Madison, Wisc., 1967), p. 155. Thomas Chatterton (1752–70) committed suicide at seventeen. Like Henry Kirke White (1785–1806) he became a Romantic representative of the poet killed by society's neglect.

[14] *Ibid.*

[15] 'To Leigh Hunt, Esq.' (the dedicatory sonnet in *Poems* (1817)).

[16] 'Addressed to [Haydon]'.

[17] *Lectures on the English Poets* (1818), *The Complete Works* ed. P. P. Howe (1930–34), v. 161–2.

[18] *William Wordsworth: The Poems*, ed. John O. Hayden (Harmondsworth, 1977), i. 569.

[19] Text from 1814 edition, cited in *John Keats*, ed. Barnard, p. 501.

[20] *Ibid.*

[21] *William Wordsworth*, ed. Hayden, i. 580–81.

[22] For an attempt to explain the significance of the order of the poems, see Jack Stillinger, *The Hoodwinking of Madeline and Other Essays on Keats's Poetry* (Urbana, Chicago, London, 1971), pp. 1–13.

[23] See Walter H. Evert, *Aesthetic and Myth in the Poetry of Keats* (Princeton, 1965).

[24] See Stuart M. Sperry, *Keats the Poet* (Princeton, 1974), p. 77.

3. *Endymion*: 'Pretty Paganism' and 'Purgatory Blind'

[1] These range from an allegory grounded on Renaissance neo-Platonism (C. L. Finney, *The Evolution of Keats's Poetry*, Cambridge, Mass., 1936, i. 291–319) to the denial that it is an allegory at all (E. C. Pettet, *On the Poetry of John Keats*, Cambridge, 1957, pp. 127–29). For a brisk account of the varieties of readings, and an account of some of the reasons for the variety, see Jack Stillinger, 'On the Interpretation of *Endymion*: The Comedian as Letter E', *The Hoodwinking of Madeline* (Urbana, Chicago, London, 1971), pp. 14–30. See also, Walter H. Evert, *Aesthetic and Myth in the Poetry of Keats* (Princeton, 1965), pp. 88–176, and Morris Dickstein, *Keats and his Poetry: A Study in Development* (Chicago and London, 1971), pp. 53–129. None of these is wholly satisfactory, though most agree that it *is* an allegory.

[2] Christopher Ricks, *Keats and Embarrassment* (Oxford, 1974), pp. 7–8, quoting from John Bayley's 'Keats and Reality' (1962), rptd, rev., and expanded as 'Uses in Poetry', Chapter II, *The Uses of Division: Unity and Disharmony in Literature* (1976), p. 115. This revision includes a reply to Ricks.

[3] Bayley, *ibid.*, p. 124.

[4] Ricks, *Keats*, p. 9.

[5] *The Alfred*, 6 Oct. 1818. Rptd *The Young Romantics and Critical Opinion 1807–1824*, ed. Theodore Redpath (1973), p. 479.

[6] *John Keats: The Complete Poems*, ed. John Barnard (Harmondsworth, 2nd edn, 1976), p. 505.

[7] *The Keats Circle: Letters and Papers 1816–1879*, ed. Hyder E. Rollins (Cambridge, Mass., 1958), ii. 144.

[8] *Ibid.*

[9] *Letters*, i. 179 (Nov. 1817).

[10] *The Life and Letters of Joseph Severn*, ed. William Sharp (New York, 1892), p. 29.

[11] *The Pantheon: or Ancient History of the Gods* . . . (1806), pp. 6–7.

[12] *Ibid.*, p. 6.

[13] 'Mr. Angerstein's Collection', *Sketches of the Principal Picture Galleries in England* (1824), *The Complete Works of William Hazlitt*, ed. P. P. Howe (1930–34), x. 7–8.

[14] *A Grammar of Motives and a Grammar of Rhetoric* (Cleveland and New York, 1962), p. 449.

[15] On the influence of the visual arts, see Ian Jack, *Keats and the Mirror of Art* (Oxford, 1967): for this identification of the source in Poussin, see p. 157. Further, see *Keats-Shelley Memorial Bulletin*, xxxiii (1982), 12–16.

[16] See W. J. Bate, *John Keats* (Cambridge, Mass., 1963), p. 177; Miriam Allott, 'Keats's *Endymion* and Shelley's *Alastor*'; *Literature of the Romantic Period*, ed. R. T. Davies and B. G. Beatty (Liverpool, 1976), pp. 151–70; and Walter H. Evert, *Aesthetic and Myth in the Poetry of Keats* (Princeton, 1965), pp. 113–15n.

[17] In her edition of *The Poems of John Keats* (1970), p. 206, Miriam Allott cites Woodhouse's note in his own copy of *Endymion*: 'K. said, with great simplicity, "It will easily be seen what I think of the present Ministers by the beginning of the 3d Book [ll. 1–22]."' Keats's blithe belief in the passage's transparency is unwarranted. Miriam Allott notes that reactionary regimes had gained strength since the restoration of the monarchy in France (1814) and the Congress of Vienna (1814–15). She also records the similarity between these lines and Hunt's articles in *The Examiner* in August 1817. The 'empurpled vests' (line 11) of the clergy echoes Hunt's mockery of the French clergy for their recent acceptance of the 'Roman purple' of Cardinal's hats, while the reference to 'trumpets . . . and sudden cannon' (lines 17–18) is likely to refer to the peace celebrations in London which followed Napoleon's abdication and culminated on 1 August 1814. Further, though Allott does not make the point, the 'idiot blink' (line 6) seems to refer to the mad George III, and the following lines to his ministers' (the 'Fire-branded foxes' of line 7) destruction of the hopes raised by the Peace, and to their disastrous refusal to allay distress caused by

poor harvests. The act passed in 1815 prohibited the import of foreign corn until wheat had reached famine prices:

> . . . O torturing fact! –
> Who, through an idiot blink, will see unpacked
> Fire-branded foxes to sear up and singe
> Our gold and ripe-eared hopes.

[18] This passage is even more obscure than Book III's attack on the Ministry. Rhadamanthus, one of the judges of the underworld whose function, says Lemprière, was 'obliging the dead to confess their crimes, and in punishing them for their offences', is set against the Golden Age of the overthrown Saturn and its innocent sexuality. The puzzling reference to Prometheus seems to invert the conventional meaning. Lemprière says, 'Prometheus made the first man and woman that ever were upon the earth, with clay, which he animated with fire which he had stolen from heaven.' Keats sees the 'dusk religion' as based on a theft, and 'Promethean clay' suggests that the god has visited his own lonely suffering onto humanity. Coming at a strategic point as the poem ends, the identification of the 'dusk religion' with contemporary middle class attitudes would support the whole poem's argument for light and freedom.

[19] See *Romantics, Rebels, and Reactionaries; English Literature and its Background 1760–1830* (Oxford, 1981), 130–31, 134–7, and 'Myth and Myth-making in the Shelley Circle', *English Literary History*, xlix (1982), 50–72.

[20] If the testimony of Walter Cooper Dendy is to be believed, and it seems unlikely in the extreme that he would have invented it, Keats scribbled out the beginning of a 'Spenserian' romance while listening to Astley Cooper lecture at St Thomas's hospital: it ends, 'The authore was goynge onne withouten discrybynge ye ladye's breste, whenne lo, a genyus appearyd – "Cuthberte", sayeth he, "an thou canst not descrybe ye ladye's brest, and fynde a simile thereunto, I forbyde thee to proceede in thy romaunt." Thys, I kenned fulle weele, far surpassyd my feble powers, and forthwythe I was fayn to droppe my quille' (*The Philosophy of Mystery* (1841), p. 99, rptd in *The Poetical Works and Other Writings of John Keats*, ed. H. Buxton Forman, rev. M. Buxton Forman, New York, 1939, v. 322).

[21] *Letters*, i. 218.

[22] *Keats Circle*, ed. Rollins, i. 34–5.

[23] Quoted Tim Chilcott, *A Publisher and his Circle: The Life and Work of John Taylor, Keats's Publisher* (1972), p. 34.

[24] Cited Ricks, *Keats*, p. 78.

[25] *Ibid.*, p. 85.

[26] *Keats: The Critical Heritage*, ed. G. M. Matthews (1971), p. 35.

[27] See also *Letters*, i. 410, 412.

[28] See, for instance, the long-running series of letters describing 'A New

System of Mythology by 'Clermont' in *The Ladies' Monthly Museum; or, Polite Repository of Amusement and Instruction: being an assemblage of whatever can tend to please the fancy, interest the mind, or exalt the character of the British Fair. Improved Series*, vi–vii (1817–18), *passim*. The story of Endymion is told as follows: '[Diana's] adventure with Endymion will, perhaps, account for this relaxation from her usual severity [i.e., waiving her law of chastity in favour of the nymph Egeria]; under the names of Luna and Phoebe, she was Goddess of the Moon; and the scandalous chronicles of Olympus inform us, that the handsome, young Endymion was favoured with a visit from her every night in a cave on Mount Latmos. This young Prince, who was a descendant of Jupiter, was admitted into Olympus, but having behaved disrespectfully to Juno, he was condemned to perpetual sleep. Fifty daughters and one son were said to be the offspring of this amour' (vii. 14).

29 The young Keats enjoyed Mrs Tighe's poetry: E. V. Weller *Keats and Mary Tighe* (New York, 1928) wholly over-estimates her influence. Her poem reached a fifth edition in *Psyche, with other Poems* (1816).

30 Harold Bloom, *The Visionary Company: A Reading of English Romantic Poetry* (New York, 1961; rptd New York, 1963), p. 396.

31 *The Romantic Survival* (1957), pp. 9–10.

32 'A Few Words on Shakespeare' (1819), *Works* (Edinburgh, 1847), vii. 430 (quoted by Bate, *John Keats*, pp. 365–6n).

4. *Hyperion:* 'Colossal Grandeur'

1 *Letters*, i. 207.

2 The major part of *Hyperion* was written, it is usually thought, between September or October 1818 and December 1818. Jack Stillinger, ed., *Poems of John Keats* (Cambridge, Mass., 1978, p. 638) thinks it 'possible' that Keats 'composed some sizable part of it between the middle of March and the middle of April 1819'. But, as Stillinger himself says, the references to the poem from 22 December 1818 to 8 March 1819 are about Keats's inability to continue the poem. The earlier dating, though inferred, seems preferable. Keats's reference to 'cogitating on the Characters of saturn and Ops' on 27 October, and his need to 'plunge into abstract images' to avoid the pain of Tom's illness on 21 September (*Letters*, i. 387, 369), both suggest that *Hyperion* was uppermost in his mind in early autumn 1818.

3 To Haydon, 23 January 1818, *Letters*, i. 207.

4 For a discussion of the pictorial traditions which may have affected Keats's treatment of *Hyperion*, see Ian Jack, *Keats and the Mirror of Art* (Oxford, 1967), Chapters 9 and 10.

5 Marginal annotation in Keats's copy of *Paradise Lost*, most easily available in *John Keats The Complete Poems*, ed. John Barnard (Harmondsworth, 2nd edn, 1976), p. 522.

6 Reported in Thomas Medwin, *Life of Percy Bysshe Shelley* (1847), ii.

109–11, quoted by G. M. Matthews, *Keats: The Critical Heritage* (1971), p. 127.

[7] *John Keats*, ed. Barnard, pp. 520–1.

[8] *Ibid.*, p. 523.

[9] Cited W. J. Bate, *John Keats* (Cambridge, Mass., 1963; rptd 1967), p. 409.

[10] All these quotations are from Keats's journal-letter to the George Keatses, *Letters*, ii. 193–4. This section was written on 18 September. For its relationship to *The Fall of Hyperion*, see p. 133.

[11] Keats wrote 'Spimpicity'.

[12] *Eclectic Review* (September 1820). Rptd in *The Young Romantics and Critical Opinion 1807–1824*, ed. Theodore Redpath (1973), pp. 508–9.

[13] Quoted by Jack, *Keats*, pp. 163–4.

[14] *Ibid.*, p. 273n.

[15] *Ibid.*, pp. 166–71.

[16] Written in Woodhouse's copy of *Endymion* (quoted *John Keats*, ed. Barnard, pp. 609–10).

[17] Lionel Trilling, *The Opposing Self* (New York, 1955), p. 47.

5. Four 'Medieval' Love Stories

[1] *Letters*, ii. 162, 174.

[2] *Poetical Works and Other Writings of John Keats*, ed. H. Buxton Forman, rev. M. Buxton Forman (New York, 1939), v. 309. This passage is normally shortened when quoted, lessening its sense of agitation.

[3] *Ibid.*, p. 310. The quotation is from *Paradise Lost*.

[4] The only text for this poem is in Keats's letter to the George Keatses of 14 February 1819. There the final line is written, 'But Death intenser – Deaths is Life's high meed' (*Letters*, ii. 81). For the argument that 'Deaths' is really a possessive and should be retained, see Walter H. Evert, *Aesthetic and Myth in the Poetry of Keats* (Princeton, 1965), pp. 291–2n. That is, 'Life's high meed is ultimately claimed by Death, which is thus more intense than Life'.

[5] See *Appendix*.

[6] *The Alfred*, 6 October 1818. Rptd, *The Young Romantics and Critical Opinion 1807–1824*, ed. Theodore Redpath (1973), p. 479.

[7] *New Monthly Magazine*, September 1820. Quoted *ibid.*, p. 436.

[8] Quoted by W. J. Bate, *John Keats* (Cambridge, Mass., 1968; rptd 1967) p. 665.

[9] See, for example, Jack Stillinger, *The Hoodwinking of Madeline and Other Essays on Keats's Poetry* (Urbana, Chicago, London, 1971), pp. 66–98.

[10] *The Complete Works*, ed. P. P. Howe (1930–34) v. 82.

[11] *The Novels and Tales of the renowned John Boccaccio: the Fifth Edition, much corrected and amended* (1684), p. 182.

[12] *Keats* (1916), p. 49.

[13] Bate, *John Keats*, pp. 312–13. Among many examples of antithesis are 'The *little sweet* doth kill *much bitterness*' and 'She *weeps* alone for *pleasures* not to be'; the poem opens with a repetition, 'Fair Isabel, poor simple Isabel', and see the repetition of the first word of the line in stanzas 16, 53, and 55.

[14] *The London Magazine*, September 1820. Rptd *Young Romantics*, ed. Redpath, pp. 504–5.

[15] The stanza originally followed stanza 17. Its tone is sarcastic rather than ironic, and illustrates Keats's difficulty in controlling his material:

> Two young Orlandos far away they seem'd,
> But on a near inspect their vapid Miens –
> Very alike, – at once themselves redeem'd
> From all suspicion of Romantic spleens –
> No fault of theirs, for their good Mother dream'd
> In the longing times of Units in their teens
> Of proudly bas'd addition and of net –
> And both their backs were mark'd with tare and tret.

[16] Christopher Ricks, *Keats and Embarrassment* (Oxford, 1974), p. 99.

[17] *Keats's Craftmanship: A Study in Poetic Development* (Oxford, 1933), p. 28.

[18] *The Poems of John Keats*, ed. Jack Stillinger (Cambridge, Mass., 1978), p. 604.

[19] Robert Burton, *The Anatomy of Melancholy* (1660 ed.), p. 538.

[20] Stillinger, *Hoodwinking of Madeline*, pp. 86–7.

[21] Other readers find the image distasteful. See William Walsh, *Introduction to Keats* (1981), p. 117.

[22] *Poems*, ed. Stillinger, p. 318n.: for the revision of stanzas 35–6, see p. 314n.

[23] Earlier readings, which see the poem as a dramatisation of Keats's ideas about the imagination, are relevant. See, for instance, Earl Wasserman, *The Finer Tone* (Baltimore, Md., 1953), pp. 97–137, and R. A. Foakes, *The Romantic Assertion* (1958), pp. 85–94.

[24] Stuart M. Sperry, *Keats the Poet* (Princeton, 1974), p. 237.

[25] *The White Goddess* (1948), p. 378.

[26] Harold Bloom, *The Visionary Company* (1961; rptd New York, 1963), pp. 375–8. For the identification with the 'demon Poesy', see K. M. Wilson, *The Nightingale and the Hawk* (1964), pp. 141–2, 144.

[27] The distinction is made by Jerome McGann in 'Keats and the Historical Method in Literary Criticism', *Modern Language Notes*, xciv (1979), 1000–1007. My indebtedness to this important article will be evident, though I do not always agree with his interpretation of the evidence.

[28] 'Why four kisses – you will say – why four because I wish to restrain the headlong impetuosity of my Muse – she would have fain said 'score' without hurting the rhyme – but we must temper the

Imagination as the Critics say with Judgment. I was obliged to choose an even number that both eyes might have fair play: and to speak truly I think two a piece quite sufficient – Suppose I had said seven; there would have been three and a half a piece – a very awkward affair – and well got out of on my side –

29 In later editions, Hunt added a note saying that 'Caviare' was chosen by Keats himself (see 1834 edn for instance).

30 McGann, *Modern Language Notes*, pp. 1001, argues that 'the *Hamlet* allusion shows us that Keats means to share a mildly insolent attitude towards the literary establishment with his readers in *The Indicator*, who are presumed to represent an undebased literary sensibility.' But Hunt's account of Alain Chartier's 'La Belle Dame', which introduces Keats's pseudonymous ballad, endorses precisely the kind of 'sentimental' feelings which Keats's alterations seek to reject. Keats is out of sympathy with Hunt's sentimentality, and by implication, that of the audience in general. Nor is there any evidence that Keats's publisher excluded the ballad from the 1820 volume because it appeared in Hunt's magazine (McGann, *Modern Language Notes*, p. 1016). The decision not to include is likely to have been Keats's own.

31 Hunt's text misprints 'PAOLO' and 'PAULO' and in line 7 has 'Not unto Ida' for 'Not to pure Ida', probably a copyist's or compositor's error arising from the similar words in the next line. *The Indicator*'s text has therefore been emended. The other substantive difference is 'mid' for 'in' (line 10). For further details, see Stillinger, ed., *Poems*, pp. 326, 635–6.

32 *The Poems of John Keats*, ed. Miriam Allott (1970), p. 499.

33 McGann, *Modern Language Notes*, p. 1007.

6. The Spring Odes, 1819

1 The poems in the 1820 volume are ordered as follows – Advertisement (saying that *Hyperion* is 'unfinished' and printed against Keats's wishes); 'Lamia', 'Isabella'; or, 'The Pot of Basil, A Story from Boccacio'; 'The Eve of St Agnes'; 'Poems' (i.e., 'Ode to a Nightingale', 'Ode on a Grecian Urn', 'Ode to Psyche', 'Fancy', 'Bards of Passion', 'Lines on the Mermaid Tavern', 'Robin Hood', 'To Autumn', 'Ode on Melancholy'); 'Hyperion. A Fragment'. 'Fancy' exists in a longer version (*Letters*, ii. 21–4). The published version may be another example of Taylor's interference.

2 September 1820. Rptd, *The Young Romantics and Critical Opinion 1807–1824*, ed. Theodore Redpath (1973), pp. 506–8.

3 Jack Stillinger, *The Poems of John Keats* (Cambridge, Mass., 1978), p. 647, says 'probably composed towards the end of April 1819'.

4 'If by dull rhymes our English must be chain'd', line 5.

5 For a fuller account of the parallel and of the relation of the ode to Keats's earlier poetry and his response to painting, see 'Keats's Tactile

Vision: "Ode to Psyche" and the Early Poetry', *Keats-Shelley Memorial Bulletin*, xxxiii (1982), 1–24.

[6] See Kenneth Allott, 'The "Ode to Psyche"', *John Keats: A Reassessment*, ed. Kenneth Allott (Liverpool, 1958), pp. 74–94, an important and formative account.

[7] See further lines 181–96 in Milton's poem.

[8] Harold Bloom comments, 'It takes an effort to recollect that these mountains and other phenomena are all within the mind' (*The Visionary Company* (New York, 1961; rptd New York, 1963), p. 423).

[9] *Keats the Poet* (Princeton, 1973), pp. 258–9, 261.

[10] 'Missing the Sea', *Selected Poetry*, ed. Wayne Brown (1981), p. 21.

[11] Keats clearly drew on Lemprière's account of Psyche, which makes the usual neo-Platonic identification of the goddess with the soul, in writing the poem.

[12] Earl Wasserman, *The Finer Tone* (Baltimore, Md., 1953), p. 60. See also J. Middleton Murry, *Keats* (1955), pp. 210–26.

[13] The most elegant account of this aspect of the poem is still Cleanth Brooks's 'Keats's Sylvan Historian: History without Footnotes', *The Well-Wrought Urn* (New York, 1947), pp. 139–52.

[14] My discussion is indebted to Leo Spitzer, 'The "Ode on a Grecian Urn", or Content vs Meta-Grammar,' *Comparative Literature*, vii (1955), pp. 203–25, and to John Jones, *John Keats's Dream of Truth* (1969), pp. 219–26. Spitzer connects the Ode with the tradition of ekphrasis, referring to examples both from classical Greek and German literature (ranging from Goethe to Rilke).

[15] For a brief account of, and guide to, the varying interpretations of the last two lines of the ode, see Jack Stillinger, *The Hoodwinking of Madeline and Other Essays on Keats's Poetry* (Urbana, Chicago, London, 1971), pp. 167–73.

[16] *Keats*, p. 276.

[17] 'Poetry as Menace and Atonement', *The Lords of Limit: Essays on Literature and Ideas* (1984), p. 5.

[18] *Letters*, i. 242.

[19] *Seven Types of Ambiguity* (1930; Harmondsworth, Peregrine, 1961), pp. 214–17. See also Bloom's comments on the rejected first stanza in *Visionary Company*, p. 433. This clearly mocks the self-conscious pursuer of fashionable 'melancholy' –

> Though you should build a bark of dead men's bones,
>   And rear a phantom gibbet for a mast,
> Stitch creeds together for a sail, with groans
>   To fill it out, bloodstained and aghast;
> Although your rudder be a Dragon's tail,
>   Long sever'd, yet still hard with agony,
>   Your cordage large uprootings from the skull
> Of bald Medusa; certes you would fail

> To find the Melancholy, whether she
> Dreameth in any isle of Lethe dull.

[20] Raymond Klibansky, Erwin Panofsky, Fritz Saxl, *Saturn and Melancholy. Studies in History of Natural Philosophy* (1964).

[21] That is, late May or before 9 June 1819 (*Letters*, ii. 78–9). Stillinger, ed., *Poems*, p. 655, says 'Written in spring 1819 . . . and certainly before . . . 9 June', noting the close parallel between the ode and a passage in a letter dated 19 March. But the internal evidence places the ode as a reply to 'Ode on a Grecian Urn', and there seems no reason to distrust the references to 'summer-indolence' and to May (line 46) by Indolence's narrator (line 16).

7. Final Poems

[1] W. H. Evert, *Aesthetic and Myth in the Poetry of Keats* (Princeton, 1965), pp. 276–81.

[2] *The Indicator*, 2 and 9 August 1820. Rptd in *The Young Romantics and Critical Opinion 1807–1824*, ed. Theodore Redpath (1973), p. 497.

[3] September 1820, *ibid.*, p. 500.

[4] See Appendix.

[5] The only factual evidence for dating 'Bright star' is the record on Brown's transcript that it was written in 1819. The manuscript evidence associates it firmly with Fanny Brawne. Long regarded as Keats's last poem, an earlier date seems certain. Robert Gittings's conjectural date of October 1818 is unlikely. The parallel between *Letters*, ii. 133, and the star imagery in the sonnet, suggest 2 July 1819 as a possible date. A date between October and December 1819 is also possible, given the similarities in images with the other poems to Fanny. Jack Stillinger, *The Poems of John Keats* (Cambridge, Mass., 1978), although he says dating is entirely speculative, gives it a chronological place in April 1819. I now think that it must have been written at a different time from the other Fanny poems, and would place it earlier than in my edition of *John Keats: The Complete Poems* (Harmondsworth, 2nd edn, 1976), probably in early July 1819.

[6] The significance of the 'full draught . . . parent of my theme' (I. 41–51) is obscure. It is taken involuntarily, and the dreamer struggles hard against its effects. The draught, stronger than opium or assassins' poison, should perhaps be identified with the involuntary awareness of suffering, the 'dark passages' when 'We see not the ballance of good and evil' (*Letters*, i. 281).

[7] See *The Poems of John Keats*, ed. Miriam Allott (1970), pp. 662–3nn.

[8] A three, or, more probably, a four-fold distinction seems to be made. Unimaginative men simply sleep their lives away, but would die if exposed to the dreamer's experience (I. 150–54). Men, who feel the agony of the world but who 'labour for mortal good', are content with

humanity (I. 156–65). Only 'dreamers' or true poets need to enter either the arbour or the temple, but they differ absolutely in kind (I. 166–81). For a useful summary of earlier views and a sensible reading, see Morris Dickstein, *Keats and His Poetry: A Study in Development* (Chicago, London, 1974), pp. 250–51.

9 F. R. Leavis, *Revaluation: Tradition and Development in English Poetry* (1936), p. 271.

10 See Geoffrey Hartman, 'Spectral Symbolism and the Authorial Self: An Approach to Keats's *Hyperion*', *Essays in Criticism*, xxiv (1974), 1–19. See also Frank Kermode, *Romantic Image* (1957, rptd., 1971), pp. 19–22.

11 *Romantics, Rebels and Reactionaries: English Literature and its Background 1760–1830* (Oxford, 1981), p. 153.

12 See the whole discussion, *ibid.*, pp. 151–4.

13 See *Letters*, ii. 194.

14 As seems implied by Butler, *Romantics*, pp. 151–2.

15 Keats's belief in the inevitability of progress was severely questioned by the poverty and suffering he saw in Scotland and, in particular, in Ireland during the late summer of 1818 (*Letters*, i. 321) – 'What a tremendous difficulty is the improvement of the condition of such people – I cannot conceive how a mind "with child" of Philanthropy could gra[s]p at possibility – with me it is absolute despair'.

16 For a close and informed account of Keats's thinking about religion, see Robert M. Ryan, *Keats: The Religious Sense* (Princeton, 1976).

17 Butler, *Romantics*, p. 152, identifies the 'fanatic' of line 1 with Wordsworth's Wanderer in *The Excursion* (1814). Wordsworth may well have been in Keats's mind, but the prime target is religious superstition.

18 See J. Livingston Lowes, 'Moneta's Temple', *Publications of the Modern Language Association of America*, li (1936), 1106–13. The 'chafing-dish' suggests that Keats has other ancient religions in mind.

19 In *John Keats*, p. 675, I identified Autumn as a female figure. I was wrong. If any further proof is needed, see the remarkable female conjured up by Bloom's 'male' misprision in *The Visionary Company* (New York, 1961), pp. 452–4. However, Helen Vendler also takes Autumn to be female: see *The Odes of John Keats* (Cambridge, Mass., 1983), pp. 227ff.

20 Ian Jack, *Keats and the Mirror of Art* (Oxford, 1967), pp. 232–5, gives examples reaching back to Keats's earliest poetry.

21 For example, see William Kent's engraving for 'Autumn' in the 1730 edition of Thomson's *Seasons*. It is conveniently reproduced in *The Seasons and The Castle of Indolence*, ed. James Sambrook (Oxford, 1972), p. 88.

22 My discussion is indebted to Christopher Ricks, *Keats and Embarrassment* (Oxford, 1974), pp. 205–11.

23 For these readings, see Geoffrey Hartman, 'Poem and Ideology: A Study of Keats's "To Autumn"' in *The Fate of Reading* (Chicago,

1975), pp. 124–46, and Jerome McGann, 'Keats and the Historical Method in Literary Criticism', *Modern Language Notes*, xciv (1979), 1017–24.

Conclusion

1 The phrase is John Jones, *John Keats's Dream of Truth* (1969), p. 295.
2 Tim Chilcott, *A Publisher and his Circle: The Life and Work of John Taylor, Keats's Publisher* (1972), pp. 51–2. As Chilcott points out, the timing of publication (July 1821) was singularly unfortunate. The Prince Regent's accession, his wife's return in June 1820, and his attempts to divorce her, created a crisis threatening the succession which took up the press and public attention until late autumn.
3 'I have given up Hyperion – there were too many Miltonic inversions in it – Miltonic verse cannot be written but in an artful or rather artist's humour' (*Letters*, ii. 167). See also his comments to the George Keatses, *ibid.*, p. 212.
4 A few phrases earlier Keats says, 'A Man's life of any worth is a continual allegory – and very few eyes can see the Mystery of his life' (*Letters*, ii. 67).
5 *The Letters of Percy Bysshe Shelley*, ed. F. L. Jones (Oxford, 1964), ii. 196.
6 See, for instance, Robert Gittings, *The Mask of Keats* (1956), pp. 115–43; *John Keats* (1968), pp. 368–73; and Phyllis Mann, 'Keats's Indian Allegory', *Keats-Shelley Journal*, vi (1957), 4–9.

Appendix

1 The dating of these poems is uncertain. As Jack Stillinger says, 'the specific October datings by almost all scholars are not well grounded' (*Poems of John Keats*, Cambridge, Mass., 1978, p. 673). The only MS. evidence is Brown's transcripts of two of the poems which give '1819'. My own edition is overconfident in dating these poems, which, with the exception of 'To Fanny', probably belong to the end of 1819 (*John Keats: The Complete Poems* (Harmondsworth, 2nd edn. 1976), pp. 682–4, 694).

Select reading

Texts

The Poems of John Keats, ed. Miriam Allott (1970, 2nd impression 1972). Full annotation, but text based on H. W. Garrod's outdated edition.

John Keats: The Complete Poems, ed. John Barnard (Harmondsworth, 2nd edn 1976). Annotated, and the text of the second edition corrected against Stillinger's findings in *The Texts of Keats's Poems* (Cambridge, Mass., 1974).

The Poems of John Keats, ed. Jack Stillinger (Cambridge, Mass., 1978). Based on a re-examination of the text with a full record of variants. Replaces H. W. Garrod's work. Textual annotation only.

The Letters of John Keats 1814–21, ed. Hyder E. Rollins, 2 vols. (Cambridge, Mass., 1958).

Biography

W. J. Bate, *John Keats* (Cambridge, Mass., 1963).

Robert Gittings, *John Keats* (1968).

Criticism

John Bayley, 'Uses in Poetry' in *The Uses of Division: Unity and Disharmony in Literature* (1976). An important essay.

Cleanth Brooks, 'History without Footnotes: An Account of Keats's Urn' in *The Well Wrought Urn* (New York, 1947). Remains an essential account. Frequently reprinted.

Marilyn Butler, 'The War of the Intellectuals: From Wordsworth to Keats' in *Romantic, Rebels and Reactionaries: English Literature and its Background 1760–1830* (Oxford, 1981). Vigorous and challenging contextual account of the Romantics.

Ian Jack, *Keats and the Mirror of Art* (Oxford, 1967).

John Jones, *John Keats's Dream of Truth* (1969). A very inward reading of the poetry which makes demands of its readers.

F. R. Leavis, 'Keats' in *Revaluation* (1936). An important essay.

Jerome McGann, 'Keats and the Historical Method in Literary Criticism', *Modern Language Notes*, xciv (1979).

Kenneth Muir (ed.), *John Keats: A Reassessment* (Liverpool, 1959). Contains a number of useful essays and Kenneth Allott's very good account of 'Ode to Psyche'.

SELECT READING

Christopher Ricks, *Keats and Embarrassment* (Oxford, 1974). Very good on the letters and Keats's sensibility.

M. R. Ridley, *Keats's Craftsmanship: A Study in Poetic Development* (Oxford, 1933).

Stuart M. Sperry, *Keats the Poet* (Princeton, 1974).

Jack Stillinger, *The Hoodwinking of Madeline and other Essays on Keats's Poetry* (Urbana, Chicago, London, 1971).

Helen Vendler, *The Odes of John Keats* (Cambridge, Mass., 1983).

Earl R. Wasserman, *The Finer Tone: Keats's Major Poems* (Baltimore, Md., 1953).

Index of persons and Keats's poems